Updates and Commentary on Employment Discrimination Law, 2020

Updates and Commentary on Employment Discrimination Law, 2020

Marcia L. McCormick
Professor of Law and Associate Dean for Academic Affairs
Professor of Women's and Gender Studies
Saint Louis University School of Law

Wolters Kluwer

To contact Customer Service, e-mail customer.service@wolterskluwer.com, call 1-800-234-1660, fax 1-800-901-9075, or mail correspondence to:

> Wolters Kluwer
> Attn: Order Department
> PO Box 990
> Frederick, MD 21705

Printed in the United States of America.

1 2 3 4 5 6 7 8 9 0

ISBN 978-1-5438-1592-4

About Wolters Kluwer Legal & Regulatory U.S.

Wolters Kluwer Legal & Regulatory U.S. delivers expert content and solutions in the areas of law, corporate compliance, health compliance, reimbursement, and legal education. Its practical solutions help customers successfully navigate the demands of a changing environment to drive their daily activities, enhance decision quality and inspire confident outcomes.

Serving customers worldwide, its legal and regulatory portfolio includes products under the Aspen Publishers, CCH Incorporated, Kluwer Law International, ftwilliam.com and MediRegs names. They are regarded as exceptional and trusted resources for general legal and practice-specific knowledge, compliance and risk management, dynamic workflow solutions, and expert commentary.

Contents

About the Author

Marcia L. McCormick is a Professor of Law at Saint Louis University School of Law, where she teaches Employment Discrimination, other labor and employment law courses, and constitutional law courses.

Thanks to Luke Klein for excellent research assistance.

Updates and Commentary on Employment Discrimination Law, 2020

I. Introduction

This *Employment Discrimination* update is intended primarily to cover developments that have occurred in 2019, but because it is the first of its kind, I plan to include a few important developments from 2018 that continue to impact the field. In addition, a number of developments included in this update involve cases that were not discrimination cases, but will affect employment discrimination law and litigation.

II. Coverage and Process

A. Who Is an Employer?

It's common to describe employer coverage in federal employment discrimination laws as focused on the number of employees an entity has. Title VII, for example, provides that "[t]he term 'employer' means a person engaged in an industry affecting commerce who has fifteen or more employees."[1] When it was enacted, Title VII only applied to private sector employers, but it was amended in 1972 to extend coverage to the public sector.[2] That legislation made clear that "[t]he term 'person,' includes . . . governments, governmental agencies, [and] political subdivisions" in addition to individuals and other entities previously included.[3] Thus, state and local government entities are covered by Title VII but as for private employees, only if they have 15 or more employees.

When a small Arizona Fire Department laid off its two oldest firefighters and they sued under the Age Discrimination in Employment Act (ADEA), the Department moved to dismiss the lawsuit, arguing that it was too small to be covered.[4] Resolving a circuit split on the issue, the Supreme Court unanimously held that the ADEA applies to all state and local governments entities regardless of size.[5] The primary reason that the ADEA was interpreted differently from Title VII related to the language in the ADEA's coverage provision, which is significantly different from Title VII's. The ADEA provides that "[t]he term 'employer' means a person engaged in an industry affecting commerce who has twenty or more employees. . . . The term also means (1) any agent of such a person, and (2) a State or political

---

1. 42 U.S.C. § 2000e(b) (2012).
2. Pub. L. 92-261, § 2, 86 Stat. 103 (1972).
3. *Id.* (codified at 42 U.S.C. § 2000e(a)).
4. Mount Lemmon Fire Dist. v. Guido, 139 S. Ct. 22 (2018).
5. *Id.* at 24.

subdivision of a State."[6] Instead of adding state and local governments to the definition of "person," Congress added them as an additional category to a person with twenty or more employees engaged in an industry affecting commerce.[7] This difference in language between Title VII and the ADEA, plus the plain language of the ADEA's provision, led the Court to interpret the ADEA differently from it and more like the Fair Labor Standards Act, which also forms the basis for a number of ADEA provisions.[8]

B.   The Administrative Process and Litigation

In roughly the last year, the Supreme Court issued decisions in two cases that addressed important procedural questions. One concerned whether filing a charge was a jurisdictional requirement. The other concerned what happens to limitations periods for state law claims when they are brought in federal court as supplemental to a federal claim, the federal claim is dismissed, and the federal court declines to continue to exercise jurisdiction over those state law claims.

Turning to the first case, before they can bring a civil action in state or federal court under Title VII, plaintiffs must exhaust administrative remedies by filing a charge with a state or local fair employment practices agency (if one exists) and the Equal Employment Opportunity Commission.[9] Failing to do so within the time required, or failing to allege the kind of discrimination ultimately alleged in a lawsuit can both result in dismissal of the action. Before last year, the Supreme Court had never decided whether this exhaustion requirement was jurisdictional.

In *Fort Bend County, Texas v. Davis*,[10] the Court decided it was not. The employee in that case had filled out an intake form, alleging that she had been harassed and retaliated against for reporting that harassment, and that form was translated into a charge, timely filed with the EEOC.[11] After that charge was filed, the employee was scheduled to work on a Sunday that conflicted with a church obligation. When she notified the employer and offered to find a coworker to cover, her supervisor told her that if she did not work the Sunday shift, she would be terminated. She went to church and was fired.[12] She handwrote an update to her intake form based on this discharge and failure to accommodate her religious practices, but

---

6. 29 U.S.C. § 630(b) (2012).
7. *Mount Lemmon Fire Dist.*, 139 S. Ct. at 25-26.
8. *Id.* at 25-27.
9. 42 U.S.C. § 2000e-5 (2012).
10. 139 S. Ct. 1843 (2018).
11. *Id.* at 1847.
12. *Id.*

didn't change the formal charge form. A few months later, she was issued a right to sue letter and brought a civil action for discrimination on the basis of religion and retaliation for reporting harassment.[13] Her employer was granted summary judgment on both claims, but the judgment on her religious claim was overturned on appeal.[14] On remand, the employer asserted for the first time that the employee had failed to exhaust administrative remedies for her religion claim.[15] After the district court held that the charge-filing requirement was jurisdictional, the Fifth Circuit reversed, holding that it was a prudential prerequisite that the employer waived by not raising charge-filing in a timely manner. This decision created a circuit split on the issue.[16]

Writing for a unanimous Court, Justice Ginsburg explained

> [T]he word "jurisdictional" is generally reserved for prescriptions delineating the classes of cases a court may entertain (subject-matter jurisdiction) and the persons over whom the court may exercise adjudicatory authority (personal jurisdiction).
>
> Congress may make other prescriptions jurisdictional by incorporating them into a jurisdictional provision, as Congress has done with the amount-in-controversy requirement for federal-court diversity jurisdiction. . . . In addition, the Court has stated it would treat a requirement as "jurisdictional" when "a long line of [Supreme] Cour[t] decisions left undisturbed by Congress" attached a jurisdictional label to the prescription.
>
> Characterizing a rule as a limit on subject-matter jurisdiction "renders it unique in our adversarial system." Unlike most arguments, challenges to subject-matter jurisdiction may be raised by the defendant "at any point in the litigation," and courts must consider them sua sponte. . . .
>
> The Court has . . . stressed the distinction between jurisdictional prescriptions and nonjurisdictional claim-processing rules, which "seek to promote the orderly progress of litigation by requiring that the parties take certain procedural steps at certain specified times." A claim-processing rule may be "mandatory" in the sense that a court must enforce the rule if a party "properly raise[s]" it. But an objection based on a mandatory claim-processing rule may be forfeited "if the party asserting the rule waits too long to raise the point."[17]

Because Congress did not frame the charge-filing requirement in jurisdictional language but instead included it as part of a set of

13. *Id.* at 1847-48.
14. *Id.* at 1848.
15. *Id.*
16. *Id.* The Fourth Circuit had held that the charge-filing requirement was jurisdictional. Jones v. Calvert Grp., Ltd., 551 F.3d 297, 300 (4th Cir. 2009).
17. *Id.* at 1848-49 (alterations in original).

"procedural obligations," the Court concluded that the requirement is not jurisdictional.[18]

The second case focused not on Title VII, but instead on the statutes governing federal court jurisdiction. When a plaintiff brings a federal claim in federal court, the court may exercise supplemental jurisdiction over any state law claims against in-state parties that "are so related to claims . . . within [federal-court competence] that they form part of the same case or controversy."[19] If the court dismisses the federal claims, it can also dismiss the state claims without prejudice if there is a good reason to do so. When the federal court does so, the supplemental jurisdiction statute provides that "[t]he period of limitations for any [supplemental] claim . . . shall be tolled while the claim is pending and for a period of 30 days after it is dismissed unless State law provides for a longer tolling period."[20]

The question in *Artis v. District of Columbia*[21] was whether this instruction to "toll" a state limitations period means to hold it in abeyance, i.e., to stop the clock,[22] or whether instead the limitations period continues to run, but reopens for a thirty-day grace period once the federal claim is dismissed. The plaintiff had brought an employment discrimination action, challenging her dismissal under federal law, but also raised three claims under D.C. law connected with her discharge.[23] When she brought her action, nearly two years remained of the limitations period on her state law claims.[24] About six months after the limitations period would have expired, the district court granted summary judgment for the employer on the federal claim and declined to exercise jurisdiction over the claims under D.C. law.[25] Fifty-nine days after the dismissal, the plaintiff refiled the D.C. claims in the D.C. Superior Court. The court dismissed her action as untimely, since it was filed more than thirty days after the dismissal of her federal action, and the D.C. Circuit affirmed.

In a 5-4 decision, written by Justice Ginsburg, the Supreme Court reversed. Noting that the dictionary definition of "toll" when used in connection with a limitations period means "to suspend or stop temporarily" and that this was the consistent use of the term in federal courts, the Court held that the plaintiff's claim remained timely.[26] This did not resolve the matter entirely, though. The employer argued that if the tolling provision in the supplemental jurisdiction statute stopped the clock, that provision would exceed Congress's powers, either because the power to extend the state limitations

18. *Id.* at 1851-52.
19. 28 U.S.C. § 1367 (2012).
20. *Id.* § 1367(d).
21. 138 S. Ct. 594 (2018).
22. *Id.* at 598.
23. *Id.* 599.
24. *Id.* at 600.
25. *Id.* at 599.
26. *Id.* at 601-02

period was too attenuated to an enumerated power or because doing so dictated a procedural rule for state courts' adjudication of state claims.[27] The Court rejected those arguments as well. The tolling rule is necessary and proper for carrying out Congress's power to "constitute Tribunals inferior to the Supreme Court" which could exercise the judicial power of the United States.[28] The Court further declined to reconsider precedent upholding Congress's power to enact the tolling provision on federalism grounds.[29]

Justice Gorsuch, joined by Justices Kennedy, Thomas, and Alito, dissented. Drawing on tradition, common law approaches, and alternative meanings of "toll," the dissent would have held that Congress intended to create a thirty-day grace period only.[30] A grace period approach, in the dissent's view, was the only one necessary to carry out the federal judicial power.[31] And the imposition on state sovereignty made that provision improper as well:[32]

> The stop clock approach . . . ensures that traditional state law judgments about the appropriate lifespan of state law claims will be routinely displaced—and displaced in favor of nothing more than a fortuity (the time a claim sits in federal court) that bears no rational relationship to any federal interest.[33]

To reinforce federalism constraints, the dissent would have held that the supplemental jurisdiction statute provided only a thirty-day grace period for refiling.[34]

C. Arbitration

Mandatory pre-dispute arbitration of employment disputes has been a hot topic, particularly in the employment discrimination context, since at least 1991, when the Supreme Court decided *Gilmer v. Interstate/Johnson Lane Corp.*,[35] holding that an ADEA claim could be subjected to compulsory arbitration. The Supreme Court has continued issuing arbitration decisions on a fairly regular basis, including four in 2018-19.

The biggest blockbuster of the four was not about arbitration per se, but involved agreements increasingly linked with arbitration agreements—class

27. *Id.* at 606.
28. *Id.* at 606-07.
29. *Id.* at 607.
30. *Id.* at 608-14 (Gorsuch, J., dissenting).
31. *Id.* at 614-16.
32. *Id.* at 616-17.
33. *Id.* at 617.
34. *Id.*
35. 500 U.S. 20 (1991).

action waivers. The Court had held in *AT&T Mobility v. Concepcion* that class action waivers in arbitration agreements were enforceable and that a state rule that such waivers would be unconscionable could not be enforced.[36] In the Court's words, "[r]equiring the availability of classwide arbitration interferes with fundamental attributes of arbitration and . . . creates a scheme inconsistent with the [purpose of the] FAA," and is thus preempted.[37]

Concepcion involved consumer contracts, rather than employment relationships, and so sources of rights that might be available to employees were not considered. Shortly after the decision, the National Labor Relations Board issued a decision that such agreements in the employment context violated the National Labor Relations Act and the Norris-LaGuardia Act by interfering with substantive worker rights to engage in concerted activity for mutual aid and protection.[38] A circuit split developed, and in *Epic Systems Corp. v. Lewis*,[39] the Court had to decide the issue. In a 5-4 decision, the Court held that class action waivers were enforceable and requiring employees to agree to them did not violate the NLRA or the Norris-LaGuardia Act.[40] The cases in which this issue was litigated were wage and hour cases, rather than discrimination cases, but the arbitration clauses at issue waived right to bring any claim connected with employment, including discrimination claims.

In April of this year, the Court followed with a decision clarifying that every arbitration clause will be interpreted to bar class claims in arbitration as well, unless the arbitration clause explicitly allows for class claims.[41] The Court stated that its conclusion followed from "a long line of cases holding that the FAA provides the default rule for resolving certain ambiguities in arbitration agreements" and that class claims were inconsistent with the "fundamental attributes" of arbitration.[42]

While these cases strengthen a tool to prevent litigation of employment claims, there are signs that employers may be rethinking the use of arbitration clauses. Employee representatives are beginning to bring mass individual arbitration claims; *Bloomberg* reported on four such campaigns in early 2019.[43] The most robust involves 12,501 claims filed by drivers against Uber, alleging they were improperly classified as independent contractors. Just to initiate these under Uber's terms, Uber will have to pay more than

36. 563 U.S. 333, 344 (2011).
37. *Id.*
38. D.R. Horton, Inc., 357 N.L.R.B. 2277 (2012).
39. 138 S. Ct. 1612 (2018).
40. *Id.* at 1623.
41. Lamps Plus, Inc. v. Varela, 139 S. Ct. 1407 (2019).
42. *Id.* at 1418-19.
43. Andrew Wallender, *Corporate Arbitration Tactic Backfires as Claims Flood in*, DAILY LAB. REP. BLOOMBERG LAW (Feb. 11, 2019, 5:06 AM), https://news.bloomberglaw.com/daily-labor-report/corporate-arbitration-tactic-backfires-as-claims-flood-in.

$18.7 million. Employers were already losing enthusiasm for arbitration according to a quoted member of the Association of Corporate Counsel, and this development may accelerate that trend. More on this trend in the context of sexual harassment claims will be discussed below.

In a break from the trend, the Court also decided that contracts with at least some transportation workers were not subject to the Federal Arbitration Act,[44] which provides that the Act cannot be used to compel arbitration of a contract of employment of a worker engaged in interstate commerce.[45] In *New Prime Inc. v. Oliveira*, an interstate trucking company tried to compel arbitration of a dispute over classification of drivers and wages in a case brought by one of its drivers. The company argued that the Act's exception did not apply, because its drivers were independent contractors. Noting that statutory terms should be interpreted according to their ordinary meaning at the time Congress enacted the statute, the Court concluded that contracts of employment in 1925 meant any kind of contract to perform work and signaled nothing about the narrower definition of employee that has evolved since that time.[46]

Justice Ginsburg wrote a brief concurring, qualifying the interpretive strategy employed in the Court's opinion:

> "[W]ords generally should be 'interpreted as taking their ordinary . . . meaning . . . at the time Congress enacted the statute.'" Ante, at 539 (quoting Wisconsin Central Ltd. v. United States, 138 S. Ct. 2067, 2074 (2018)). The Court so reaffirms, and I agree. Looking to the period of enactment to gauge statutory meaning ordinarily fosters fidelity to the "regime . . . Congress established." MCI Telecommunications Corp. v. American Telephone & Telegraph Co., 512 U.S. 218, 234, 114 S. Ct. 2223 (1994).
>
> Congress, however, may design legislation to govern changing times and circumstances. *See, e.g.*, Kimble v. Marvel Entertainment, LLC, 135 S. Ct. 2401, 2412 (2015) ("Congress . . . intended [the Sherman Antitrust Act's] reference to 'restraint of trade' to have 'changing content,' and authorized courts to oversee the term's 'dynamic potential.'" (quoting Business Electronics Corp. v. Sharp Electronics Corp., 485 U.S. 717, 731-732, 108 S. Ct. 1515 (1988))); SEC v. Zandford, 535 U.S. 813, 819, 122 S. Ct. 1899 (2002) (In enacting the Securities Exchange Act, "Congress sought to substitute a philosophy of full disclosure for the philosophy of caveat emptor . . . . Consequently, . . . the statute should be construed not technically and restrictively, but flexibly to effectuate its remedial purposes." (internal quotation marks and paragraph break omitted)); H.J. Inc. v. Northwestern Bell Telephone Co., 492 U.S. 229, 243, 109 S. Ct. 2893 (1989) ("The limits of the relationship and continuity concepts that combine to define a [Racketeer Influenced and Corrupt

44. New Prime Inc. v. Oliveira, 139 S. Ct. 532, 544 (2019).
45. 9 U.S.C. § 1 (2012).
46. *New Prime Inc.*, 139 S. Ct. at 539-40.

Organizations] pattern . . . cannot be fixed in advance with such clarity that it will always be apparent whether in a particular case a 'pattern of racketeering activity' exists. The development of these concepts must await future cases . . . ."). As these illustrations suggest, sometimes, "[w]ords in statutes can enlarge or contract their scope as other changes, in law or in the world, require their application to new instances or make old applications anachronistic." West v. Gibson, 527 U.S. 212, 218, 119 S. Ct. 1906 (1999).[47]

Her purpose in clarifying the limits on such an "original public meaning" approach was likely to create a sound basis for deviating from it in anticipation of cases pending this term on whether Title VII prohibits discrimination on the basis of sexual orientation or gender identity. These are discussed below.

New Prime Inc. is already having an effect. The Third Circuit recently held that Uber drivers might be transportation workers engaged in interstate commerce such that classification challenges do not need to be arbitrated.[48] The court did not affirmatively answer the question of whether the plaintiff and other Uber drivers were engaged in interstate commerce or sufficiently related work, but noted that the plaintiff, at least, alleged that he frequently drove passengers across state lines.[49] Instructing the lower court on remand, the Third Circuit suggested that it allow discovery and consider "a wide variety of sources, including, but not limited to and in no particular order, the contents of the parties' agreement(s), information regarding the industry in which the class of workers is engaged, information regarding the work performed by those workers, and various texts—i.e., other laws, dictionaries, and documents—that discuss the parties and the work."[50]

Legislative efforts limiting the use of arbitration in employment are underway in Congress as has been true in prior sessions. For example, in February, the Forced Arbitration Injustice Repeal (FAIR) Act, which would prohibit the enforcement of predispute arbitration agreements in consumer, employment, antitrust, or civil rights disputes, was reintroduced with 222 cosponsors in the House[51] and 34 in the Senate.[52] Legislation regarding arbitration of harassment claims will be discussed below.

47. *Id.* at 544 (Ginsburg, J., concurring).
48. Singh v. Uber Techs., Inc., No. 17-1397, ___ F.3d ___, 2019 WL 4282185 (3d Cir. Sept. 11, 2019).
49. *Id.* at *12.
50. *Id.* at *13.
51. H.R. 1423, 116th Cong. (2019).
52. S. 610, 116th Cong. (2019).

III.   *Analytical Models/Theories of Discrimination*

A.   Disparate Treatment

Courts continue to debate the proper test to determine whether a case can proceed to trial on a motion for summary judgment. The Eleventh Circuit weighed in this year in an interesting case involving a police detective in Georgia, *Lewis v. City of Union City, Georgia*.[53] Jacqueline Lewis brought a disability, race, and sex discrimination claim against the police department when she was terminated after about ten years of service.[54] She had been placed on administrative leave after she requested an accommodation from a requirement that she be trained to use a taser or pepper spray; her doctor was concerned that the training, which required officers to be subject to a five second taser shock, would cause Lewis an injury because she had suffered a mild heart attack previously.[55] Lewis was put on administrative leave and then terminated for being absent without leave.[56]

After Lewis brought an action challenging her discharge, the city moved for summary judgment. In opposition to that motion, Lewis offered two comparators, both white men, who were treated more favorably when they were not able to perform an aspect of their jobs; they were given more time to come to a solution.[57] The district court granted summary judgment, finding that the two comparators were not similar enough to Lewis.[58]

On appeal, a panel of the Eleventh Circuit reversed. It found, among other things, that Lewis had presented sufficient evidence to establish a genuine issue of material fact on her discrimination claims.[59] One judge dissented, and the full court, sitting en banc, vacated the decision in order to "clarify the proper standard for comparator evidence in intentional discrimination cases."[60] Ultimately, the court held that a plaintiff had to demonstrate that her comparators were similar in all material respects to her and that Lewis had failed to do so.[61] The court remanded the matter to the panel for further proceedings.[62] The panel, on reconsideration, held that Lewis had nonetheless shown a genuine issue of material fact, enabling her to survive summary judgment.[63]

---

53. 918 F.3d 1213 (11th Cir. 2019) (en banc), *on remand* No. 15-11362, ___ F.3d ___, 2019 WL 3821804 (11th Cir. Aug. 15, 2019).
54. 918 F.3d at 1218-19.
55. *Id.* at 1219.
56. *Lewis*, No. 15-11362, 2019 WL 3821804, at *1, *4.
57. *Id.* at *5.
58. *Id.*
59. *Id.*
60. *Lewis*, 918 F.3d at 1220.
61. *Id.* at 1231.
62. *Id.*
63. *Lewis*, No. 15-11362, 2019 WL 3821804, at *12-13.

The most important and interesting parts of the court's decisions involved the framework to be used to analyze discrimination cases at summary judgment. That was what the en banc court sought to clarify. In the court's words,

> Faced with a defendant's motion for summary judgment, a plaintiff asserting an intentional-discrimination claim under Title VII of the Civil Rights Act of 1964, the Equal Protection Clause, or 42 U.S.C. § 1981 must make a sufficient factual showing to permit a reasonable jury to rule in her favor. She can do so in a variety of ways, one of which is by navigating the now-familiar three-part burden-shifting framework established by the Supreme Court in *McDonnell Douglas Corp. v. Green*, 411 U.S. 792, 93 S. Ct. 1817 (1973). Under that framework, the plaintiff bears the initial burden of establishing a prima facie case of discrimination by proving, among other things, that she was treated differently from another "similarly situated" individual–in court-speak, a "comparator." *Texas Dep't of Cmty. Affairs v. Burdine*, 450 U.S. 248, 258–59, 101 S. Ct. 1089 (1981) (citing McDonnell Douglas, 411 U.S. at 804, 93 S. Ct. 1817). The obvious question: Just how "similarly situated" must a plaintiff and her comparator(s) be?

> To date, our attempts to answer that question have only sown confusion. In some cases, we have required a proper comparator to be "nearly identical" to the plaintiff. *See, e.g.*, Nix v. WLCY Radio/Rahall Commc'ns, 738 F.2d 1181, 1185 (11th Cir. 1984) (citations omitted). In others, we have expressly rejected a nearly-identical standard. *See, e.g.*, Alexander v. Fulton Cty., 207 F.3d 1303, 1333–34 (11th Cir. 2000). In still others, without even mentioning the nearly-identical benchmark, we have deemed it sufficient that the plaintiff and the comparator engaged in the "same or similar" conduct. *See, e.g.*, Holifield v. Reno, 115 F.3d 1555, 1562 (11th Cir. 1997) (per curiam). And to make matters worse, in still others we have applied both the nearly-identical and same-or-similar standards simultaneously. *See, e.g.*, Maniccia v. Brown, 171 F.3d 1364, 1368 (11th Cir. 1999). It's a mess.

> In an effort to clean up, and to clarify once and for all the proper standard for comparator evidence in intentional-discrimination cases, we took this case en banc . . . .[64]

Ultimately, the court focused on at what stage in the framework evidence of a comparator had to be presented and how stringent that comparison had to be. Although the Supreme Court has never explicitly held that the *McDonnell Douglas* prima facie case *requires* evidence of a comparator, the court concluded that it essentially had:

---

64. *Lewis*, 918 F.3d at 1217-18.

For starters, the Supreme Court has repeatedly (and consistently) included a comparator-evidence assessment—using one formulation or another—as an element of a plaintiff's *prima facie* case. Beginning in *McDonnell Douglas* itself, the Court emphasized that a Title VII plaintiff—there bringing a failure-to-hire claim—carries his *prima facie* burden "by showing (i) that he belongs to a racial minority; (ii) that he applied and was qualified for a job for which the employer was seeking applicants; (iii) that, despite his qualifications, he was rejected; and"—importantly here—"(iv) that, after his rejection, the position remained open and the employer continued to seek applicants from persons of complainant's qualifications." 411 U.S. at 802, 93 S. Ct. 1817. The Court reiterated a similar four-part *prima facie* test in *Furnco Construction Corp. v. Waters*, 438 U.S. 567, 575, 98 S. Ct. 2943 (1978), and again in *St. Mary's Honor Center v. Hicks*, 509 U.S. at 506, 113 S. Ct. 2742. Most recently, in *Young v. United Parcel Service, Inc.*, the Court applied the *McDonnell Douglas* framework to a failure-to-accommodate claim arising under the Pregnancy Discrimination Act, and in so doing restated yet again the required four-step test: "[A] plaintiff . . . may make out a *prima facie* case by showing, as in *McDonnell Douglas*, [1] that she belongs to the protected class, [2] that she sought accommodation, [3] that the employer did not accommodate her, and [4] that the employer did accommodate others 'similar in their ability or inability to work.' " —— U.S. ——, 135 S. Ct. 1338, 1354 (2015) (enumeration added).

The Supreme Court has located the comparator analysis in *McDonnell Douglas*'s preliminary stage for good reason. Lest we forget, the plaintiff's burden at step one is to show a *prima facie* case of something in particular—namely, unlawful intentional "discrimination." *See, e.g., McDonnell Douglas*, 411 U.S. at 802, 93 S. Ct. 1817 ("The complainant in a Title VII trial must carry the initial burden under the statute of establishing a *prima facie* case of racial *discrimination*." (emphasis added)); *Burdine*, 450 U.S. at 252–53, 101 S. Ct. 1089 ("discrimination"); *St. Mary's*, 509 U.S. at 506, 113 S. Ct. 2742 ("discrimination"). "The *prima facie* case serves an important function," the Supreme Court has said, in that "it eliminates the most common nondiscriminatory reasons" for the employer's treatment of the plaintiff—and in so doing "give[s] rise to an inference of unlawful discrimination." *Burdine*, 450 U.S. at 253–54, 101 S. Ct. 1089; *see also Furnco*, 438 U.S. at 577, 98 S. Ct. 2943 (same); *Int'l Bhd. of Teamsters v. United States*, 431 U.S. 324, 358, 97 S. Ct. 1843 (1977) (same). A successful *prima facie* showing thus establishes a "legally mandatory, rebuttable presumption" of intentional discrimination, *Burdine*, 450 U.S. at 254 n.7, 101 S. Ct. 1089, that "produces a required conclusion in the absence of explanation" by the employer, *St. Mary's*, 509 U.S. at 506, 113 S. Ct. 2742 (quotation marks omitted). In other words, establishing a *prima facie* case of discrimination entitles the plaintiff to judgment—to victory—if the employer either can't, won't, or doesn't provide a nondiscriminatory explanation for its actions. *See Burdine*, 450 U.S. at 254, 101 S. Ct. 1089 ("[I]f the employer is silent in the face of the presumption, the court must enter judgment for the plaintiff because no issue of fact remains in the case."). It follows, therefore, that at the *prima facie* stage the plaintiff must show a potential "winner"—*i.e.*, enough to give rise to a valid inference that her employer engaged in unlawful intentional "discrimination."

So what exactly is this "discrimination," an inference of which is the object of the plaintiff's *prima facie* case? As we have said many times—and as all of us know intuitively—"[d]iscrimination consists of *treating like cases differently.*" *N.L.R.B. v. Collier*, 553 F.2d 425, 428 (5th Cir. 1977) (emphasis added); *see also, e.g., Frosty Morn Meats, Inc. v. N.L.R.B.*, 296 F.2d 617, 621 (5th Cir. 1961). The converse, of course, is also true: Treating *different* cases differently is not discriminatory, let alone intentionally so. *See Nix v. WLCY Radio/Rahall Commc'ns*, 738 F.2d 1181, 1186 (11th Cir. 1984) ("[I]f an employer applies a rule differently to people it believes are *differently* situated, no discriminatory intent has been shown.") (quoting *Chescheir v. Liberty Mut. Ins. Co.*, 713 F.2d 1142, 1148 (5th Cir. 1983)) (emphasis added).

By its very nature, therefore, discrimination is a comparative concept—it requires an assessment of whether "like" (or instead different) people or things are being treated "differently." In light of that reality—and because a sufficient *prima facie* showing gives rise to an inference of unlawful discrimination—"mov[ing]" the comparator analysis out of the initial *prima facie* stage and into the tertiary pretext stage, as Lewis requests, would make no sense. Were we to do so, a plaintiff could demonstrate a potential winner at step one by showing only (1) that she belongs to a protected class, (2) that she suffered some adverse employment action, and (3) that she was qualified to perform the job in question. But even conclusive proof of those three elements can't entitle a plaintiff to judgment on a claim for unlawful *discrimination*. Absent a qualitative comparison at the *prima facie* stage—*i.e.*, without determining whether the employer treated like cases differently—there's no way of knowing (or even inferring) that discrimination is afoot. Think about it: Every qualified minority employee who gets fired, for instance, necessarily satisfies the first three prongs of the traditional *prima facie* case. But that employee could have been terminated because she was chronically late, because she had a foul mouth, or for any of a number of other nondiscriminatory reasons. It is only by demonstrating that her employer has treated "like" employees "differently"—*i.e.*, through an assessment of comparators—that a plaintiff can supply the missing link and provide a valid basis for inferring unlawful *discrimination*.

You see the problem: Lewis's proposal that the qualitative assessment of comparator evidence be "move[d]" out of the *prima facie* stage and into the pretext stage would allow the plaintiff to proceed—and potentially to win—without *any* good ground for presuming that discrimination has occurred. Doing so would effectively shift to the defendant the burden of *disproving* discrimination—which is precisely what the Supreme Court has forbidden. *See, e.g., Burdine*, 450 U.S. at 253, 254–58, 101 S. Ct. 1089 (rejecting rules that placed too stringent a burden on a gender-discrimination defendant and emphasizing that the "ultimate burden of persuading the trier of fact that the defendant intentionally discriminated against the plaintiff remains at all times with the plaintiff").[9]

[9] We reject Lewis's (and the dissent's) suggestion that *McDonnell Douglas* itself somehow indicates that the analysis of comparators should be relegated to the tertiary pretext stage. While it's true that the Court there

considered at the pretext phase whether white employees had engaged in conduct of "comparable seriousness" to the African-American plaintiff's, that fact alone says nothing about the propriety—or in light of subsequent Supreme Court precedent, necessity—of conducting a comparative analysis as part of the *prima facie* stage. Evidence necessary and proper to support a plaintiff's *prima facie* case may of course be used, later as it were, to demonstrate that the defendant's explanation for its conduct was pretextual. *See, e.g., Reeves v. Sanderson Plumbing Prods., Inc.,* 530 U.S. 133, 143, 120 S. Ct. 2097 (2000) (observing that "although the presumption of discrimination 'drops out of the picture' once the defendant meets its burden of production, . . . the trier of fact may still consider the evidence establishing the plaintiff's prima facie case and 'inferences properly drawn therefrom . . . on the issue of whether the defendant's explanation is pretextual'") (quoting *Burdine,* 450 U.S. at 255, 101 S. Ct. 1089).

* * *

We have no trouble concluding, therefore, that a meaningful comparator analysis must remain part of the *prima facie* case. In order to defeat summary judgment, a Title VII plaintiff proceeding under *McDonnell Douglas* must prove, as a preliminary matter, not only that she is a member of a protected class, that she suffered an adverse employment action, and that she was qualified for the job in question, but also that she was treated less favorably than "similarly situated" individuals outside her class.[65]

The court went on to consider how similar comparators must be, ultimately holding that "a plaintiff must show that she and her comparators are 'similarly situated in all material respects.'"[66] In reaching that conclusion, the court stated,

we take as our lodestars (1) the ordinary meaning of the term "discrimination" and (2) the twin policies that the Supreme Court has said animate the *McDonnell Douglas* framework's *prima facie* case. First, "discrimination": Discrimination, as we have explained, is the act of "treating *like* cases differently." Quintessential discrimination—the Platonic form, if you will—therefore requires true "like[ness]," perfect apples-to-apples identity. As Lewis and her amici correctly explain, however, in the real world (and real workplaces) "doppelgangers are like unicorns"—they don't exist. So practically speaking, at least, perfect identity is a non-starter. But in adopting a comparator standard, we must not stray too far from paradigmatic notions of discrimination, lest we sanction a regime in which treating *different* things differently violates Title VII, which clearly it does not. Second, and relatedly, we must be mindful of the two functions that the Supreme Court has said the *prima facie* case is designed to serve—(1) to eliminate "the most common nondiscriminatory reasons" for an employer's conduct, and (2) to provide a sound basis for an

65. *Id.* at 1221-24.
66. *Id.* at 1224.

"inference of unlawful discrimination." *Burdine*, 450 U.S. at 253–54, 101 S. Ct. 1089; *see also Furnco*, 438 U.S. at 577, 98 S. Ct. 2943; *Young*, 135 S. Ct. at 1354.

It's clear, we think, that [the Seventh Circuit's "flexible, common-sense"] standard—which . . . deems the similarly-situated standard satisfied "[s]o long as the distinctions between the plaintiff and the proposed comparators are not 'so significant that they render the comparison effectively useless'" [*Coleman v. Donahoe*, 667 F.3d 835, 846 (7th Cir. 2012)]—fails these tests. In its looseness, [this] standard departs too dramatically from the essential sameness that is necessary to a preliminary determination that the plaintiff's employer has engaged in unlawful "discrimination." A plaintiff and a comparator might be alike in some (even random) sense, such that a comparison wouldn't necessarily be irrelevant or crazy. But without closer correspondence, the comparison wouldn't provide any sound basis for eliminating legitimate reasons for an employer's conduct or validly inferring discriminatory animus.

Separately, [this] standard risks giving courts too much leeway to upset employers' valid business judgments. In applying *McDonnell Douglas*, the Supreme Court has stressed the importance of striking an appropriate balance between employee protection and employer discretion. In *McKennon v. Nashville Banner Publishing Co.*, for instance, the Court observed that federal antidiscrimination statutes do "not constrain employers from exercising significant other prerogatives and discretions in the course of the hiring, promoting, and discharging of their employees," and emphasized that courts deciding cases arising under those laws "must recognize" not only "the important claims of the employee[s]" but also "the legitimate interests of the employer." 513 U.S. 352, 361, 115 S. Ct. 879 (1995). The reason for deference, the Court has explained, is that "[c]ourts are generally less competent than employers to restructure business practices, and unless mandated to do so by Congress they should not attempt it." *Furnco*, 438 U.S. at 578, 98 S. Ct. 2943. By permitting cases to proceed on the most meager showing of similarity between a plaintiff and her comparators, [this] not-useless standard would thrust courts into staffing decisions that bear no meaningful indicia of unlawful discrimination.

Finally, it seems to us inevitable that [this standard] would effectively eliminate summary judgment as a tool for winnowing out meritless claims. Indeed, forestalling summary judgment appears to be a feature of the not-useless standard, not a bug. . . . Without prejudging, it seems to us inconceivable . . . that nearly every one of the hundreds of Title VII cases filed in this Circuit last year warranted a full trial.

While [this] standard is clearly too lenient, the [nearly identical standard] is too strict—or at least has the appearance of being too strict. Although we have employed it for some time now–albeit inconsistently–the nearly-identical standard gives off the wrong "vibe." Despite the adverb "nearly"–and our repeated reassurances that "comparators need not be the plaintiff's doppelgangers," *Flowers v. Troup County, Georgia, School District*, 803 F.3d 1327, 1340 (11th Cir. 2015), and, even more explicitly, that " '[n]early identical' . . . does not mean 'exactly identical,' " *McCann v. Tillman*, 526 F.3d 1370, 1374 n.4

(11th Cir. 2008)–there is a risk that litigants, commentators, and (worst of all) courts have come to believe that it requires something akin to doppelganger-like sameness. Although we must take care not to venture too far from the form — "apples should be compared to apples" — we must also remember that "[e]xact correlation is neither likely nor necessary." *Dartmouth Review v. Dartmouth Coll.*, 889 F.2d 13, 19 (1st Cir. 1989), *overruled on other grounds by Educadores Puertorriqueños en Acción v. Hernandez*, 367 F.3d 61 (1st Cir. 2004). And we are not willing to take the risk that the nearly-identical test is causing courts reflexively to dismiss potentially valid antidiscrimination cases.[67]

To help guide future courts, the court explained that to be similar, a comparator should have engaged in the same basic kind of conduct as the plaintiff, have been subject to the same employment policy or rule as the plaintiff, and likely will have been subject to the same decisionmaker as the plaintiff.[68] Applying this standard to Lewis's facts, the court held that her comparators were not similarly situated in all material respects because they were placed on leave years apart, under different personnel policies, for different conditions.[69]

Given this holding, readers might be surprised that the panel on remand nonetheless held that Lewis's case survived summary judgment. The panel analyzed her allegations under a framework alternative to the *McDonnell Douglas* test: the convincing mosaic test originally adopted by the Seventh Circuit.

> "[E]stablishing the elements of the *McDonnell Douglas* framework is not, and never was intended to be, the *sine qua non* for a plaintiff to survive a summary judgment motion in an employment discrimination case. Accordingly, the plaintiff's failure to produce a comparator does not necessarily doom the plaintiff's case." *Smith v. Lockheed-Martin Corp.*, 644 F.3d 1321, 1328 (11th Cir. 2011). Even without similarly situated comparators, "the plaintiff will always survive summary judgment if he [or she] presents circumstantial evidence that creates a triable issue concerning the employer's discriminatory intent." *Id.*

> This, of course, is perfectly logical. Not every employee subjected to unlawful discrimination will be able to produce a similarly situated comparator. Among other things, a proper comparator simply may not exist in every workplace. Accordingly, a "plaintiff will always survive summary judgment if he presents . . . 'a convincing mosaic of circumstantial evidence that would allow a jury to infer intentional discrimination.'" *Id.* (quoting *Silverman v. Bd. of Educ. of City of Chi.*, 637 F.3d 729, 734 (7th Cir. 2011), *overruled by Ortiz v. Werner Enters., Inc.*, 834 F.3d 760 (7th Cir. 2016) (footnote omitted)). A "convincing mosaic" may be shown by evidence that demonstrates, among other things, (1) "suspicious timing, ambiguous statements . . . , and other bits and

---

67. *Id.* at 1225-27.
68. *Id.* at 1227-28.
69. *Id.* at 1230.

pieces from which an inference of discriminatory intent might be drawn," (2) systematically better treatment of similarly situated employees, and (3) that the employer's justification is pretextual. *Silverman*, 637 F.3d at 733-34 (quotations omitted).[70]

Because the en banc court had noted that the convincing mosaic standard was an alternative available to a plaintiff,[71] it is a bit curious that the court took the case en banc at all. Not surprisingly, the employer has filed another petition for rehearing en banc, arguing among other things that the convincing mosaic standard as applied requires a defendant to disprove discriminatory motive.[72]

This case and other developments in the *McDonnell Douglas* framework are quite thoroughly discussed in Sandra Sperino's book, MCDONNELL DOUGLAS: THE MOST IMPORTANT CASE IN EMPLOYMENT DISCRIMINATION LAW (Bloomberg), the second edition of which is forthcoming. Sandra summarized several important developments, including the *Lewis* case, in the *Friend of the Court* Blog last May.[73] She also highlighted Katie Eyer's recent article, *The Return of the Technical* McDonnell Douglas *Paradigm*.[74]

As the Eleventh Circuit's discussion shows, this struggle over the frameworks and applicable standard in disparate treatment cases is really a struggle over what behavior and state of mind counts as discrimination. It is also a struggle over the question of how common discrimination is. Courts seem skeptical that discrimination continues to occur at a high enough rate that it is likely explanation for a decision that seems arbitrary.

B.   Mixed Motives

After the decisions in *Gross v. FBL Financial Services*[75] and *University of Texas Southwest Medical Center v. Nassar*,[76] which held that plaintiffs must prove but-for causation under the Age Discrimination in Employment Act and Title VII's retaliation provisions, respectively, courts have been considering whether that standard also must be used in Americans with Disabilities Act cases, or whether a motivating factor standard applies. In April, the Second Circuit held in *Natofsky v. City of New York* that but-for causation was

70. *Lewis*, No. 15-11362, 2019 WL 3821804, at *11-12.
71. *Lewis*, 918 F.3d at 1220 n.6.
72. Defendants Appellees' Petition for Rehearing en banc, *Lewis*, No. 15-11362, 2019 WL 3821804.
73. *Top 5* McDonell Douglas *Updates*, FRIEND OF THE COURT (May 23, 2019), https://friend-ofthecourtblog.wordpress.com/2019/05/23/top-5-mcdonnell-douglas-updates/.
74. 94 WASH. L. REV. ___ (forthcoming 2019), (draft available at https://papers.ssrn.com/sol3/papers.cfm?abstract_id=3362529).
75. 557 U.S. 167, 129 S. Ct. 2343 (2009).
76. 570 U.S. 338, 133 S. Ct. 2517 (2013).

required.[77] The court rested its conclusion on two primary reasons: (1) the ADA does not contain a causation standard like that in Title VII, which uses the phrase "motivating factor," and (2) there is no reason to interpret "based on," the language used in the ADA, differently from "because of," the language used in the ADEA and Title VII's retaliation provision.[78] The Second Circuit thus joins the Fourth,[79] Sixth,[80] and Seventh Circuits[81] in requiring but-for causation. Judge Chin dissented, noting that the motivating factor standard had been used under the ADA for more than twenty years and was in use when Congress enacted the ADA Amendments Act, restoring a broad interpretation of the ADA.[82]

The issue continues to evolve. Legislation has been introduced in Congress to amend the ADEA, Title VII, and the ADA to provide that the causation standard for each should be motivating factor.[83] In addition, the Supreme Court is set to consider the applicable causation standard to be used in race discrimination cases brought under 42 U.S.C. § 1981 in *Comcast Corp. v. National Association of African American-Owned Media*.[84] Relying on the language of § 1981, which guarantees to all "the same right" to contract "as is enjoyed by white citizens," the Ninth Circuit had held that if race played any role in a decision, it violated that statute.[85] The Second[86] and Third[87] Circuits had issued decisions using a mixed motives proof structure previously.

C.   Disparate Impact

Two particularly significant disparate impact cases were decided by circuit courts in the last year. In one, the Fifth Circuit curtailed the effects of the EEOC's efforts to use disparate impact to address use of criminal record information in employment decisions. In the other, the Seventh Circuit held that disparate impact cases could not be brought under the ADEA by applicants, but only current employees.

---

77. 921 F.3d 337 (2d Cir. 2019).
78. *Id.* at 348-49.
79. Gentry v. E.W. Partners Club Mgmt. Co. Inc., 816 F.3d 228, 235–36 (4th Cir. 2016).
80. Lewis v. Humboldt Acquisition Corp., 681 F.3d 312, 321 (6th Cir. 2012).
81. Serwatka v. Rockwell Automation, Inc., 591 F.3d 957, 963–64 (7th Cir. 2010).
82. *Natofsky*, 921 F.3d at 354-56 (Chin, J. dissenting).
83. Protecting Older Workers against Discrimination Act, H.R. 1230, 116th Cong. (2019).
84. No. 18-1711.
85. Nat'l Ass'n of African American-Owned Media v. Charter Commc'ns, 915 F.3d 617, 626 (9th Cir.2019) (en banc).
86. Garcia v. Hartford Police Dep't, 706 F.3d 120, 127 (2d Cir.2013).
87. Brown v. J. Kaz, Inc., 581 F.3d 175, 192 n.5 (3d Cir. 2009)

i.   *Criminal Records*

In 2012, the EEOC issued guidance on the use of arrest and conviction records in employment decisions, cautioning that such use could cause a disparate impact on the basis of race and national origin because of disparities in the criminal justice system on the basis of race and national origin.[88] That guidance provided, in part,

> With respect to criminal records, there is Title VII disparate impact liability where the evidence shows that a covered employer's criminal record screening policy or practice disproportionately screens out a Title VII-protected group and the employer does not demonstrate that the policy or practice is job related for the positions in question and consistent with business necessity.[89]

The guidance essentially suggested that because national data suggested that there was a disparity in criminal justice on the basis of race and national origin, the Commission would presume that any employment decisions made on the basis of arrest or conviction records would have the same impact, unless during the investigation an employer could show that its particular use did not have a disparate impact.[90] If the employer could not do so, it would have to show that its use of arrest or conviction records effectively "link[ed] specific criminal conduct, and its dangers, with the risks inherent in the duties of a particular position," by, for example, validating the policy, or by making an individualized assessment of the particular criminal conduct and the nature of the job.[91]

The state of Texas challenged that guidance in 2013 as beyond the EEOC's authority, bringing a declaratory judgment action in federal court.[92] Texas bars people with felony convictions from a number of jobs with state agencies.[93] After a series of lower court decisions and a prior appeal, the Fifth Circuit held that the EEOC's guidance was a final agency action subject to the Administrative Procedure Act and that it was not enforceable.[94] The court noted early in the opinion that "EEOC has limited rulemaking and enforcement power with respect to Title VII. It may issue only 'procedural regulations' implementing Title VII and may not promulgate substantive

---

88. EEOC Enforcement Guidance 915.002 (2012), https://www.eeoc.gov/laws/guidance/upload/arrest_conviction.pdf.
89. *Id.* at 9.
90. *Id.* at 10.
91. *Id.* at 14.
92. Texas v. Equal Emp't Opportunity Comm'n, 933 F.3d 433, 439-40 (2019).
93. *Id.* at 439.
94. *Id.* at 446, 450-51.

rules."[95] From that starting point, the court ultimately concluded, "Because the Guidance is a substantive rule, and the text of Title VII and precedent confirm that EEOC lacks authority to promulgate substantive rules implementing Title VII," the EEOC and Attorney General would be enjoined from enforcing the rule against the state of Texas.[96]

The practical effect of this injunction is a little unclear. Although the injunction only limits enforcement against one group of employers in one state, the logic of the decision would suggest that the guidance, and in fact any substantive guidance issued by the EEOC is unenforceable. At the same time, it appears that the EEOC could, independent of the guidance, conduct an investigation of a charge alleging disparate impact discrimination on this ground, and the Department of Justice could bring an action against the state challenging its policy. The Department would just have to prove the disparate impact in that case instead of relying on the presumption in the rule.

ii.   ADEA and Applicants

In early 2019, The Seventh Circuit, sitting en banc, issued a decision, limiting the reach of disparate impact under the ADEA. An edited version follows:

Kleber v. CareFusion Corp.

914 F.3d 480 (7th Cir. 2019) (en banc)

SCUDDER, Circuit Judge.

After Dale Kleber unsuccessfully applied for a job at CareFusion Corporation, he sued for age discrimination on a theory of disparate impact liability. The district court dismissed his claim, concluding that § 4(a)(2) of the Age Discrimination in Employment Act did not authorize job applicants like Kleber to bring a disparate impact claim against a prospective employer. A divided panel of this court reversed. We granted en banc review and, affirming the district court, now hold that the plain language of § 4(a)(2) makes clear that Congress, while protecting employees from disparate impact age discrimination, did not extend that same protection to outside job applicants. While our conclusion is grounded in § 4(a)(2)'s plain language, it is reinforced by the ADEA's broader structure and history.

---

95. *Id.* at 439 (citing See 42 U.S.C. § 2000e-12(a); EEOC v. Arabian Am. Oil Co., 499 U.S. 244, 257, 111 S. Ct. 1227 (1991)).
96. *Id.* at 450-51.

I

In March 2014, Kleber, an attorney, applied for a senior in-house position in CareFusion's law department. The job description required applicants to have "3 to 7 years (no more than 7 years) of relevant legal experience." Kleber was 58 at the time he applied and had more than seven years of pertinent experience. CareFusion passed over Kleber and instead hired a 29-year-old applicant who met but did not exceed the prescribed experience requirement.

* * *

II

A

We begin with the plain language of § 4(a)(2). "If the statutory language is plain, we must enforce it according to its terms." This precept reinforces the constitutional principle of separation of powers, for our role is to interpret the words Congress enacts into law without altering a statute's clear limits.

Section 4(a)(2) makes it unlawful for an employer

> to limit, segregate, or classify his employees in any way which would deprive or tend to deprive any individual of employment opportunities or otherwise adversely affect his status as an employee, because of such individual's age.

29 U.S.C. § 623(a)(2).

By its terms, § 4(a)(2) proscribes certain conduct by employers and limits its protection to employees. The prohibited conduct entails an employer acting in any way to limit, segregate, or classify its employees based on age. The language of § 4(a)(2) then goes on to make clear that its proscriptions apply only if an employer's actions have a particular impact—"depriv[ing] or tend[ing] to deprive any individual of employment opportunities or otherwise adversely affect[ing] his status as an employee." This language plainly demonstrates that the requisite impact must befall an individual with "status as an employee." Put most simply, the reach of § 4(a)(2) does not extend to applicants for employment, as common dictionary definitions confirm that an applicant has no "status as an employee." *See* Merriam-Webster's Collegiate Dictionary 60, 408 (11th ed. 2003) (defining "applicant" as "one who applies," including, for example, "a job [applicant]," while defining "employee" as "one employed by another usu[ally] for wages or salary and in a position below the executive level").

Subjecting the language of § 4(a)(2) to even closer scrutiny reinforces our conclusion. Congress did not prohibit just conduct that "would deprive or tend to deprive any individual of employment opportunities." It went further. Section 4(a)(2) employs a catchall formulation—"or otherwise adversely affect his status as an employee"—to extend the proscribed conduct.

Congress's word choice is significant and has a unifying effect: the use of "or otherwise" serves to stitch the prohibitions and scope of § 4(a)(2) into a whole, first by making clear that the proscribed acts cover all conduct "otherwise affect[ing] his status as an employee," and, second, by limiting the reach of the statutory protection to an individual with "status as an employee." See *Villarreal v. R.J. Reynolds Tobacco Co.*, 839 F.3d 958, 964 (11th Cir. 2016) (en banc) (interpreting § 4(a)(2) the same way and explaining that the "or otherwise" language "operates as a catchall: the specific items that precede it are meant to be subsumed by what comes after the 'or otherwise'").

Kleber begs to differ, arguing that § 4(a)(2)'s coverage extends beyond employees to applicants for employment. He gets there by focusing on the language in the middle of § 4(a)(2) — "deprive or tend to deprive any individual of employment opportunities" — and contends that the use of the expansive term "any individual" shows that Congress wished to cover outside job applicants. If the only question were whether a job applicant counts as "any individual," Kleber would be right. But time and again the Supreme Court has instructed that statutory interpretation requires reading a text as a whole, and here that requires that we refrain from isolating two words when the language surrounding those two words supplies essential meaning and resolves the question before us.

Reading § 4(a)(2) in its entirety shows that Congress employed the term "any individual" as a shorthand reference to someone with "status as an employee." This construction is clear from Congress's use of language telling us that the provision covers "any individual" deprived of an employment opportunity because such conduct "adversely affects his status as an employee." Put differently, ordinary principles of grammatical construction require connecting "any individual" (the antecedent) with the subsequent personal possessive pronoun "his," and upon doing so we naturally read "any individual" as referring and limited to someone with "status as an employee." The clear takeaway is that a covered individual must be an employee.

Our conclusion becomes ironclad the moment we look beyond § 4(a)(2) and ask whether other provisions of the ADEA distinguish between employees and applicants. We do not have to look far to see that the answer is yes.

Right next door to § 4(a)(2) is § 4(a)(1), the ADEA's disparate treatment provision. In § 4(a)(1), Congress made it unlawful for an employer "to fail or refuse to hire or to discharge any individual or otherwise discriminate against any individual with respect to his compensation, terms, conditions, or privileges of employment, because of such individual's age." 29 U.S.C. § 623(a)(1) (emphasis added). All agree that § 4(a)(1), by its terms, covers both employees and applicants. Compelling this consensus is § 4(a)(1)'s use of the words "to fail or refuse to hire or to discharge," which make clear that "any individual" includes someone seeking to be hired.

Yet a side-by-side comparison of § 4(a)(1) with § 4(a)(2) shows that the language in the former plainly covering applicants is conspicuously absent from the latter. Section 4(a)(2) says nothing about an employer's decision "to fail or refuse to hire . . . any individual" and instead speaks only in terms of an employer's actions that "adversely affect his status as an employee." We cannot conclude this difference means nothing: "when 'Congress includes particular language in one section of a statute but omits it in another'—let alone in the very next provision—the Court presumes that Congress intended a difference in meaning."

There is even more. A short distance away from § 4(a)(2) is § 4(c)(2), which disallows labor organizations from engaging in particular conduct. Section 4(c)(2), in pertinent part, makes it unlawful for a labor organization

> to limit, segregate, or classify its membership . . . in any way which would deprive or tend to deprive any individual of employment opportunities . . . or otherwise adversely affect his status as an employee *or as an applicant for employment*, because of such individual's age.

29 U.S.C. § 623(c)(2) (emphasis added).

* * *

Consider yet another example. In § 4(d), Congress addressed employer retaliation by making it "unlawful for an employer to discriminate against any of his employees *or applicants for employment*" because such an individual has opposed certain unlawful practices of age discrimination. 29 U.S.C. § 623(d) (emphasis added). Here, too, the distinction between "employees" and "applicants" jumps off the page.

Each of these provisions distinguishes between employees and applicants. It is implausible that Congress intended no such distinction in § 4(a)(2), however, and instead used the term employees to cover both employees and applicants. To conclude otherwise runs afoul of the Supreme Court's admonition to take statutes as we find them by giving effect to differences in meaning evidenced by differences in language.

In the end, the plain language of § 4(a)(2) leaves room for only one interpretation: Congress authorized only employees to bring disparate impact claims.

B

Kleber urges a different conclusion in no small part on the basis of the Supreme Court's 1971 decision in *Griggs v. Duke Power Co.*, 401 U.S. 424, where the Court interpreted § 703(a)(2) of Title VII and held that disparate impact was a viable theory of liability. Indeed, Kleber goes so far as to say *Griggs*—a case where the Court considered language in Title VII that at the time paralleled the language we consider here—controls and mandates a decision in his favor. We disagree.

A commonsense observation is warranted at the outset. If Kleber is right that *Griggs*, a Title VII case, compels the conclusion that § 4(a)(2) of the

ADEA authorizes outside job applicants to bring a disparate impact claim, we find it very difficult to explain why it took the Supreme Court 34 years to resolve whether anyone—employee or applicant—could sue on a disparate impact theory under the ADEA, as it did in *Smith v. City of Jackson*, 544 U.S. 228 (2005). There was no need for the Court to decide *Smith* if (all or part of) the answer came in *Griggs*. And when the Court did decide *Smith* the Justices' separate opinions recognized the imperative of showing impact to an individual's "status as an employee" when discerning the reach of § 4(a)(2).

Kleber's position fares no better within the four corners of *Griggs* itself. . . .

Kleber would have us read *Griggs* beyond its facts by focusing on language in a couple of places in the Court's opinion that he sees as covering employees and applicants alike. We decline the invitation. Nowhere in *Griggs* did the Court state that its holding extended to job applicants. And that makes perfect sense because nothing about the case, brought as it was by employees of Duke Power and not outside applicants, required the Court to answer that question. The language that Kleber insists on reading in isolation must be read in context, and the totality of the *Griggs* opinion makes clear that the Court answered whether Duke Power's African-American employees could bring a claim for disparate impact liability based on practices that kept them from pursuing different, higher-paying jobs within the company.

What happened a year after *Griggs* cements our conclusion. In 1972, Congress amended § 703(a)(2) of Title VII—the provision at issue in *Griggs*—by adding language to expressly include "applicants for employment." Pub. L. No. 92-261, § 8(a), 86 Stat. 109 (1972). This amendment occurred in the immediate wake of *Griggs* and, in this way, reflected Congress's swift and clear desire to extend Title VII's disparate impact protection to job applicants. There was no need for Congress to amend § 703(a)(2) if the provision had always covered job applicants and especially if the Supreme Court had just said so in *Griggs*. To conclude otherwise renders the 1972 amendment a meaningless act of the 92nd Congress, and we are reluctant to conclude that substantive changes to statutes reflect idle acts.

The Supreme Court endorsed this precise course of analysis—giving effect to "Congress's decision to amend Title VII's relevant provisions but not make similar changes to the ADEA"—in *Gross v. FBL Financial Servs., Inc.*, 557 U.S. 167, 174 (2009). . . .

And so it is here. Congress's choice to add "applicants" to § 703(a)(2) of Title VII but not to amend § 4(a)(2) of the ADEA in the same way is meaningful. *Gross* teaches that we cannot ignore such differences in language between the two enactments. And, at the risk of understatement, *Gross* is far from an aberration in statutory construction. A mountain of precedent supports giving effect to statutory amendments.

* * *

C

Beyond his reliance on *Griggs*, Kleber invites us to read the ADEA against the backdrop of Congress's clear purpose of broadly prohibiting age discrimination. On this score, he points us to the Supreme Court's decision in *Robinson v. Shell Oil Company*, 519 U.S. 337 (1997) and to the report of the former Secretary of the Department of Labor, Willard Wirtz.

In *Robinson*, the Court held that § 704(a) of Title VII extended not just to "employees" (a term used in § 704(a)), but also to former employees. The Court emphasized that, while the meaning of "employees" was ambiguous, Title VII's broader structure made plain that Congress intended the term to cover former employees, a construction that furthered Title VII's broader purposes. None of this helps Kleber. (Indeed, if anything, *Robinson*'s clear observation of the distinct and separate meaning of "employees" and "applicants for employment" in § 704(a) severely undermines Kleber's textual argument.) *Robinson*, in short, provides direction on how courts—if confronted with statutory ambiguity—should resolve such ambiguity. There being no ambiguity in the meaning of § 4(a)(2) of the ADEA, our role ends—an outcome on all fours with *Robinson*.

The Wirtz Report reflected the Labor Department's response to Congress's request for recommended age discrimination legislation, and a plurality of the Supreme Court in *Smith* treated the Report as an authoritative signal of Congress's intent when enacting the ADEA. We do too.

Nobody disputes that the Wirtz Report reinforces Congress's clear aim of enacting the ADEA to prevent age discrimination in the workplace by encouraging the employment of older persons, including older job applicants. But we decline to resolve the question presented here on the basis of broad statutory purposes or, more specifically, to force an interpretation of but one provision of the ADEA (here, § 4(a)(2)) to advance the enactment's full objectives.

Our responsibility is to interpret § 4(a)(2) as it stands in the U.S. Code and to ask whether the provision covers outside job applicants. We cannot say it does and remain faithful to the provision's plain meaning. It remains the province of Congress to choose where to draw legislative lines and to mark those lines with language. Our holding gives effect to the plain limits embodied in the text of § 4(a)(2).

The ADEA, moreover, is a wide-ranging statutory scheme, made up of many provisions beyond § 4(a)(2). And a broader look at the statute shows that outside job applicants have other provisions at their disposal to respond to age discrimination. Section 4(a)(1), for example, prevents an employer from disparately treating both job applicants and employees on the basis of age. Section 4(c)(2), prevents a labor organization's potential age discrimination against both job applicants and employees.

Today's decision, while unfavorable to Kleber, leaves teeth in § 4(a)(2). The provision protects older employees who encounter age-based disparate impact discrimination in the workplace. And Congress, of course, remains free to do what the judiciary cannot—extend § 4(a)(2) to outside job applicants, as it did in amending Title VII.

For these reasons, we AFFIRM.

EASTERBROOK, Circuit Judge, dissenting.

I do not join the majority's opinion, because the statute lacks a plain meaning. *Robinson v. Shell Oil Corp.*, 519 U.S. 337 (1997), held that the word "employees" in one part of Title VII includes ex-employees. *Robinson* interpreted text in context. Here, too, the judiciary must look outside one subsection to tell whether "individual" in 29 U.S.C. § 623(a)(2) includes applicants for employment.

But neither do I join all of Judge Hamilton's dissent, which relies on legislative purpose. The purpose of a law is imputed by judges; it is not a thing to be mined out of a statute. Even when we know what direction the legislature wanted to move, we must know how far to go—and making that choice is a legislative task. Our job is to apply the enacted text, the only thing to which the House, the Senate, and the President all subscribed, not to plumb legislators' hopes and goals.

* * *

The statutory context does not point ineluctably to one understanding. The majority does not explain why the statute would use "individual" in dramatically different ways within the space of a few words. . . .

Because neither text nor purpose offers a satisfactory solution, we should stop with precedent. *Griggs v. Duke Power Co.*, 401 U.S. 424 (1971), treats the word "individual" in 42 U.S.C. § 2000e–2(a)(2), as it stood before an amendment in 1972, as including applicants for employment. The pre-1972 version of that statute is identical to the existing text in § 623(a); Congress copied this part of the ADEA from that part of Title VII. It may be that the Court in *Griggs* was careless to treat outside applicants for employment as "individuals" in paragraph (2), but that is what the Justices did. Part II of Judge Hamilton's opinion shows how this came to happen and also shows that many of the Supreme Court's later decisions read *Griggs* to hold that paragraph (2) in the pre-1972 version of Title VII applies disparate-impact theory to outside applicants for employment. If the Justices think that this topic (or *Smith* itself) needs a new look, the matter is for them to decide. I therefore join Part II of Judge Hamilton's dissenting opinion.

[Judge Hamilton wrote a nineteen-page dissent, only a tiny bit of which is reproduced here. He was joined by Chief Judge Wood and Judge Rovner. Judge Easterbrook joined as to one part]

We should hold that the disparate-impact language in § 623(a)(2) protects both outside job applicants and current employees. Part I of this opinion explains why that's the better reading of the statutory text that is at worst ambiguous on coverage of job applicants. While other ADEA provisions protect job applicants more clearly, the Supreme Court guides us away from the majority's word-matching and toward a more sensible and less arbitrary reading. See *Robinson v. Shell Oil Co.*, 519 U.S. 337, 341–46 (1997).

Part II explains that protecting outside job applicants tracks the Supreme Court's reading of identical statutory language in Title VII of the Civil Rights Act of 1964. In *Griggs v. Duke Power Co.*, 401 U.S. 424, 426 n.1 (1971), the Court found that this same disparate-treatment language protects not only current employees but also "the job-seeker"—people like plaintiff Kleber. We should read the same language the same way. The majority tries to avoid this reasoning by narrowing *Griggs* and attributing significance to the 1972 amendment of the Title VII disparate-impact provision. As detailed in Part II, the actual facts of both the *Griggs* litigation and the 1972 amendment flatly contradict the majority's glib and unsupported theories.

Part III explains that protecting both outside applicants and current employees is also more consistent with the purpose of the Act (as set forth in the statute itself) and avoids drawing an utterly arbitrary line. Neither the defendant nor its amici have offered a plausible policy reason why Congress might have chosen to allow disparate-impact claims by current employees, including internal job applicants, while excluding outside job applicants. The en banc majority does not even try to do so, following instead a deliberately naïve approach to an ambiguous statutory text, closing its eyes to fifty years of history, context, and application.

* * *

Start with the critical statutory language, which includes two parallel provisions that prohibit employers from engaging in certain behavior. Under paragraph (a)(1), an employer may not intentionally discriminate against an older individual by firing or failing to hire or promote her because she is older—i.e., engage in disparate treatment of older individuals. Paragraph (a)(2) prohibits an employer from creating an internal employee classification or limitation that has the effect of depriving "any individual of employment opportunities" or adversely affecting his or her status as an employee because of age—i.e., creating an internal classification system with a disparate impact against older individuals.

If an employer classifies a position as one that must be filled by someone with certain minimum or maximum experience requirements, it is classifying its employees within the meaning of paragraph (a)(2). If that classification "would deprive or tend to deprive any individual of employment opportunities" because of the person's age, paragraph (a)(2) can reach that classification. The broad phrase "any individual" reaches job applicants, so the focus turns to the employer's action and its effects—i.e., whether the employer has classified jobs in a way that tends to limit any individual's employment opportunities based on age. The defendant's maximum-experi-ence requirement in this case certainly limited plaintiff Kleber's employment opportunities.

* * *

The majority's analysis nullifies the two uses of the broad word "individual," which certainly reaches job applicants. What Congress meant to say, the majority argues, is that it's unlawful for an employer "to limit, segregate, or classify his employees in any way which would deprive or tend to deprive any current employee [not "any individual"] of employment opportunities or otherwise adversely affect his status as an employee, because of such employ-ee's [not "individual's"] age."

How does one read a bar against depriving "any individual" of "employment opportunities" to exclude all cases where a person is looking for a job? And if Congress meant to limit the provision's coverage only to current employees, why didn't it just use the word "employee"? It had used that word twice in this provision already. Courts are generally loath to read statutory terms out of a textual provision and to insert limitations that are not evident in the text.

* * *

. . . [E]ven if "status as an employee" must be affected to state a disparate-impact claim under (a)(2), the majority's conclusion also depends entirely on the unlikely notion that "status as an employee" is not "adversely affected" when an employer denies an individual the opportunity to become an employee in the first place. Refusing to hire an individual has the most dra-matic possible adverse effect on that individual's "status as an employee." Reading "status as an employee" broadly, to include whether the individual is an employee or not, is consistent with the actual words Congress used in repeatedly referring to "individuals," and with ordinary usage. Courts often speak of "denying status" of one sort or another. And the word "status" is not necessarily limited to status as of any particular moment. 1 U.S.C. § 1 (Dictionary Act providing that "unless the context indicates otherwise . . . words used in the present tense include the future as well as the present").

* * *

In short, the effect of the phrase "otherwise adversely affects his status as an employee" on job applicants is at worst ambiguous for applicants like Kleber. The majority loads onto that phrase more weight than it can bear. If Congress really meant to exclude job applicants from disparate-impact protection, the phrase "status as an employee" was a remarkably obscure and even obtuse way to express that meaning.

[The dissent went on to discuss the other provisions of the ADEA, the *Griggs* opinion and its effects, and the purpose of the ADEA].

Kleber, represented in part by attorneys with the American Association of Retired Persons (AARP) Foundation, filed a petition for certiorari from this decision, and that petition is scheduled to be considered by the Court in conference in October. The docket number is 18-1346.

D. Harassment

The #MeToo movement continued to have significant effects in issues connected to harassment in the workplace. A number of symposia and articles on the subject have been published in the last year or so. The Yale Law Journal[97] and the Stanford Law Review[98] jointly held symposia in the summer of 2018, collecting work by a number of scholars on the ways that harassment is linked to inequality at work and in society. The symposium produced an *Open Statement on Sexual Harassment from Employment Discrimination Law Scholars* that provided ten principles for addressing harassment.[99] A non-exhaustive list of a number of thought-provoking works include:

- Daniel Hemel & Dorothy S. Lund, *Sexual Harassment and Corporate Law*, 118 COLUM. L. REV. 1583 (2018) (examining corporate and securities law approaches to regulate and remedy workplace harassment).
- Elizabeth C. Tippett, *The Legal Implications of the MeToo Movement*, 103 MINN. L. REV. 229 (2018) (providing an overview of likely future developments)
- Lesley Wexler, Jennifer K. Robbennolt & Colleen Murphy, *#MeToo, Time's Up, and Theories of Justice*, 2019 U. ILL. L. REV. 45 (describing transitional justice approaches to remedying harassment)
- Rebecca Hanner White, *Title VII and the #MeToo Movement*, 68 EMORY L.J. ONLINE 1014 (2018) (describing the disconnect between popular understandings of harassment and legal remedies).

A number of legislative reforms have been proposed, and some were adopted at the federal and state level. The "Bringing an End to Harassment by Enhancing Accountability and Rejecting Discrimination in the Workplace Act" or the "BE HEARD in the Workplace Act," would provide a comprehensive approach to addressing harassment, providing funds for research, requiring nondiscrimination policies and training, and extending rights

---

97. 128 YALE L.J. FORUM (2018), https://www.yalelawjournal.org/collection/MeToo.

98. 71 STAN. L. REV. ONLINE (2018), https://www.stanfordlawreview.org/online/type/symposium-metoo/.

99. 71 STAN. L. REV. ONLINE 17 (2018), https://review.law.stanford.edu/wp-content/uploads/sites/3/2018/06/71-Stan.-L.-Rev.-Online-Schultz-2.pdf.

to workers not covered by Title VII.[100] Additionally, according to a report by the National Women's Law Center,

> to date, **15 states** have passed new protections. New York City has also been particularly active in strengthening its anti-harassment laws and is thus highlighted in this report.
>
> - **13 states limited or prohibit employers** from requiring employees to sign nondisclosure agreements as a condition of employment or as part of a settlement agreement.
> - **5 states expanded workplace harassment protections** to include independent contractors, interns, or graduate students for the first time.
> - **4 states and New York City extended their statute of limitations** for filing harassment or discrimination claim.
> - **10 states and New York City enacted key prevention measures**, including mandatory training and policy requirements for employers.[101]

The fifteen states include Arizona, California, Connecticut, Delaware, Illinois, Louisiana, Maryland, New Jersey, New York, Nevada, Oregon, Tennessee, Virginia, Vermont, and Washington.

IV.   Hot Topics in Protected Classes and Defenses

A.   Race

The fight to have discrimination on the basis of natural hairstyles recognized as race discrimination heated up in 2019. Two states passed the Creating a Respectful and Open World for Natural Hair (CROWN Act), prohibiting discrimination on the basis of natural hairstyles including braids, locs, and twists. California was the first,[102] and New York followed shortly after.[103] Before the new legislation was signed, New York City's Commission on Human Rights had issued guidelines, making clear that discrimination on the basis of hairstyle was race discrimination prohibited

---

100. H.R. 2148, 116th Cong. (2019).

101. NAT'L WOMEN'S LAW CTR., PROGRESS IN ADVANCING ME TOO WORKPLACE REFORMS IN #20STATESBY2020, at 2 (2019), https://nwlc-ciw49tixgw5lbab.stackpathdns.com/wp-content/uploads/2019/07/20-States-By-2020-report.pdf.

102. S.B. 188 (2019), https://leginfo.legislature.ca.gov/faces/billTextClient.xhtml?bill_id=201920200SB188.

103. S.B 6209A, A.B. 7797A (2019), https://legislation.nysenate.gov/pdf/bills/2019/S6209A.

by the New York City Human Rights Law.[104] This guidance cited D. Wendy Greene, *Splitting Hairs: The Eleventh Circuit's Take on Workplace Bans Against Black Women's Natural Hair in* EEOC v. Catastrophe Management Solutions, 71 U. Miami L. Rev. 987, 999-1000 (2017). Professor Greene has a book forthcoming on this topic, #FreeTheHair: Locking Black Hair to Civil Rights Movements (U.C. Berkeley Press).

B.   Sexual Orientation/Gender Identity

One of the fastest moving issues in the country involves the rights of sexual minorities: Lesbians, gay men, bisexuals, transgender individuals, intersex individuals, asexuals and others. As social views about what sex, gender, gender identity, and sexual orientation are and whether they are immutable have evolved, so has our view of legal policy. Much of the recent litigation on these rights has focused on access to marriage for same sex couples, but there has been a significant uptick in employment discrimination cases as well. Although early cases found no protection for transgender employees or against discrimination on the basis of sexual orientation, the Court's decision in *Price Waterhouse v. Hopkins* created opportunities to argue that discrimination on these grounds is sex discrimination. That is the EEOC's current view, and it has aggressively pursued that position:

- http://www.eeoc.gov/eeoc/newsroom/wysk/enforcement_protections_ lgbt_workers.cfm,
- http://www.eeoc.gov/eeoc/newsroom/wysk/lgbt_examples_deci- sions.cfm,
- http://www.eeoc.gov/eeoc/litigation/selected/lgbt_facts.cfm

The Supreme Court is currently considering three consolidated cases, *Bostock v. Clayton County*,[105] *Georgia, Altitude Express v. Zarda*,[106] and *R.G. & G.R. Harris Funeral Homes v. EEOC*,[107] about whether Title VII prohibits dis- crimination on the basis of sexual orientation or gender identity. Up until

104. N.Y.C. Comm'n on Human Rights, Legal Enforcement Guidance on Race Discrimination on the Basis of Hair (2019), https://www1.nyc.gov/assets/cchr/downloads/ pdf/Hair-Guidance.pdf.

105. No. 17-1618. The Supreme Court's docket with pdf versions of the documents filed in this case can be found at https://www.supremecourt.gov/search.aspx?filename=/docket/ docketfiles/html/public/17-1618.html.

106. No. 17-1623. The Supreme Court's docket with pdf versions of the documents filed in this case can be found at https://www.supremecourt.gov/search.aspx?filename=/docket/ docketfiles/html/public/17-1623.html.

107. No. 18-107. The Supreme Court's docket with pdf versions of the documents filed in this case can be found at https://www.supremecourt.gov/search.aspx?filename=/docket/ docketfiles/html/public/18-107.html.

2015, the answer to the question about whether sexual orientation discrimination violated Title VII would have mostly been "No," although courts
were having an increasingly difficult time distinguishing sex discrimination from sexual orientation discrimination, which often involved sex stereotypes. Then, in July 2015, the EEOC issued a ruling in a federal sector
case that concluded that Title VII is appropriately interpreted to protect
against discrimination on the basis of sexual orientation. *Baldwin v. Foxx*,
EEOC Appeal No. 0120133080 (July 15, 2015). About a year later, in *Hively
v. Ivy Tech Community College*, a panel of the Seventh Circuit considered the
substance of the EEOC's *Baldwin* opinion and largely agreed with the reasoning. 830 F.3d 698 (7th Cir. 2016). The panel was bound by the Seventh
Circuit's earlier decisions, though, and could not recognize the cause of
action in that case. The full Seventh Circuit reheard the case en banc and
largely adopted the EEOC's reasoning, holding that sexual orientation discrimination violated Title VII's prohibition on sex discrimination. *Hively
v. Ivy Tech. Cmty. Coll.*, 853 F.3d 339 (7th Cir.2017) (en banc). The Second
Circuit followed closely behind with *Zarda v. Altitude Express*,[108] and shortly
after that, the Eleventh Circuit, in a short panel opinion in *Bostock v. Clayton
County Board of Commissioners*,[109] rejected a sexual orientation discrimination
claim under Title VII, holding that it was bound by prior Eleventh Circuit
precedent. An edited version of *Zarda* is reproduced below. The decision
was fairly fractured, but the portions excerpted constituted the portion of
the opinion joined by a majority of justices and part of one of the dissents.

Zarda v. Altitude Express

883 F.3d 100 (2d Cir. 2018) (en banc).

KATZMANN, Chief Judge:

Donald Zarda, a skydiving instructor, brought a sex discrimination claim
under Title VII of the Civil Rights Act of 1964 ("Title VII") alleging that he was
fired from his job at Altitude Express, Inc., because he failed to conform to
male sex stereotypes by referring to his sexual orientation. Although it is well-
settled that gender stereotyping violates Title VII's prohibition on discrimination "because of . . . sex," we have previously held that sexual orientation
discrimination claims, including claims that being gay or lesbian constitutes
nonconformity with a gender stereotype, are not cognizable under Title VII.
See Simonton v. Runyon, 232 F.3d 33, 35 (2d Cir.2000); *see also Dawson v. Bumble
& Bumble*, 398 F.3d 211, 217–23 (2d Cir.2005).

At the time *Simonton* and *Dawson* were decided, and for many years since,
this view was consistent with the consensus among our sister circuits and

---

108. 883 F.3d 100 (2d Cir. 2018) (en banc), *cert. granted*, 139 S. Ct. 1599 (2019).
109. 723 F. App'x 964 (11th Cir. 2018) (mem), *cert granted*, 139 S. Ct. 1599 (2019).

the position of the Equal Employment Opportunity Commission ("EEOC" or "Commission"). But legal doctrine evolves and in 2015 the EEOC held, for the first time, that "sexual orientation is inherently a 'sex-based consideration;' accordingly an allegation of discrimination based on sexual orientation is necessarily an allegation of sex discrimination under Title VII." *Baldwin v. Foxx,* EEOC Decision No. 0120133080, 2015 WL 4397641, at *5 (July 15, 2015) (quoting *Price Waterhouse v. Hopkins,* 490 U.S. 228, 242 (1989) (plurality opinion)). Since then, two circuits have revisited the question of whether claims of sexual orientation discrimination are viable under Title VII. In March 2017, a divided panel of the Eleventh Circuit declined to recognize such a claim, concluding that it was bound by [a prior panel opinion], which "ha[s] not been overruled by a clearly contrary opinion of the Supreme Court or of [the Eleventh Circuit] sitting en banc." *Evans v. Ga. Reg'l Hosp.,* 850 F.3d 1248, 1257 (11th Cir.), cert. denied, — U.S. ——, 138 S. Ct. 557 (2017). One month later, the Seventh Circuit, sitting en banc, took "a fresh look at [its] position in light of developments at the Supreme Court extending over two decades" and held that "discrimination on the basis of sexual orientation is a form of sex discrimination." [*Hively v. Ivy Tech Cmty. Coll.,* 853 F.3d 339, 340–41 (7th Cir.2017)]. In addition, a concurring opinion of this Court recently called "for the Court to revisit" this question, emphasizing the "changing legal landscape that has taken shape in the nearly two decades since Simonton issued," and identifying multiple arguments that support the conclusion that sexual orientation discrimination is barred by Title VII. *Christiansen v. Omnicom Grp., Inc.,* 852 F.3d 195, 202 (2d Cir.2017) (Katzmann, *C.J.,* concurring).

[Sitting en banc,] we now hold that Title VII prohibits discrimination on the basis of sexual orientation as discrimination "because of . . . sex." To the extent that our prior precedents held otherwise, they are overruled.

* * *

III. SUMMARY

Since 1964, the legal framework for evaluating Title VII claims has evolved substantially. Under *Manhart,* traits that operate as a proxy for sex are an impermissible basis for disparate treatment of men and women. Under *Price Waterhouse,* discrimination on the basis of sex stereotypes is prohibited. Under [*Holcomb v. Iona College,* 521 F.3d 130 (2d Cir.2008)], building on [*Loving v. Virginia,* 388 U.S. 1, 87 S. Ct. 1817 (1967)], it is unlawful to discriminate on the basis of an employee's association with persons of another race. Applying these precedents to sexual orientation discrimination, it is clear that there is "no justification in the statutory language . . . for a categorical rule excluding" such claims from the reach of Title VII.

Title VII's prohibition on sex discrimination applies to any practice in which sex is a motivating factor. . . . [S]exual orientation discrimination is a subset of sex discrimination because sexual orientation is *defined* by one's sex in relation to the sex of those to whom one is attracted, making it impossible for an employer to discriminate on the basis of sexual orientation without taking sex into account. [But for this employee's sex, his attraction to men would not have been a firing offense]. Sexual orientation discrimination is also based on assumptions or stereotypes about how members of a particular gender should be, including to whom they should be attracted. Finally, sexual orientation discrimination is associational discrimination because an adverse employment action that is motivated by the employer's opposition to association between members of particular sexes discriminates against an employee on the basis of sex. Each of these three perspectives is sufficient to support this Court's conclusion and together they amply demonstrate that sexual orientation discrimination is a form of sex discrimination.

Although sexual orientation discrimination is "assuredly not the principal evil that Congress was concerned with when it enacted Title VII," "statutory prohibitions often go beyond the principal evil to cover reasonably comparable evils." [*Oncale v. Sundowner Offshore Servs., Inc.*, 523 U.S. 75, 79, 118 S. Ct. 998, 1002 (1998)]. In the context of Title VII, the statutory prohibition extends to all discrimination "because of . . . sex" and sexual orientation discrimination is an actionable subset of sex discrimination. We overturn our prior precedents to the contrary to the extent they conflict with this ruling.

* * *

Zarda has alleged that, by "honestly referr[ing] to his sexual orientation," he failed to "conform to the straight male macho stereotype." For this reason, he has alleged a claim of discrimination of the kind we now hold cognizable under Title VII. . . .

GERARD E. LYNCH, Circuit Judge, dissenting

Speaking solely as a citizen, I would be delighted to awake one morning and learn that Congress had just passed legislation adding sexual orientation to the list of grounds of employment discrimination prohibited under Title VII of the Civil Rights Act of 1964. I am confident that one day—and I hope that day comes soon—I will have that pleasure.

I would be equally pleased to awake to learn that Congress had secretly passed such legislation more than a half century ago—until I actually woke up and realized that I must have been still asleep and dreaming. Because we all know that Congress did no such thing.

* * *

[Regardless of the strange way that sex was added to Title VII, Congress clearly intended to prohibit discrimination against women]. Discrimination against gay women and men, by contrast, was not on the table for public debate. In those dark, pre-Stonewall days, same-sex sexual relations were criminalized in nearly all states. . . .

In addition to criminalization, gay men and women were stigmatized as suffering from mental illness. In 1964, both the American Psychiatric Association and the American Psychological Association regrettably classified homosexuality as a mental illness or disorder. . . . Because gay identity was viewed as a mental illness and was, in effect, defined by participation in a criminal act, the employment situation for openly gay Americans was bleak.

* * *

Given the criminalization of same-sex relationships and arbitrary and abusive police harassment of gay and lesbian citizens, nascent gay rights organizations had more urgent concerns than private employment discrimination. As late as 1968, four years *after* the passage of Title VII, the North American Conference of Homophile Organizations proposed a "Homosexual Bill of Rights" that demanded five fundamental rights: that private consensual sex between adults not be a crime; that solicitation of sex acts not be prosecuted except on a complaint by someone other than an undercover officer; that sexual orientation not be a factor in granting security clearances, visas, or citizenship; that homosexuality not be a barrier to service in the military; and that sexual orientation not affect eligibility for employment *with federal, state, or local governments*. Those proposals, which pointedly did not include a ban on private sector employment discrimination against gays, evidently had little traction with many Americans at the time. The first state to prohibit employment discrimination on the basis of sexual orientation even in the public sector was Pennsylvania, by executive order of the governor, in 1975—more than a decade after the Civil Rights Act had become law. It was not until 1982 that Wisconsin became the first state to ban both public and private sector discrimination based on sexual orientation. Massachusetts followed in 1989. Notably, as discussed more fully below, these states did so by explicit legislative action adding "sexual orientation" to pre-existing anti-discrimination laws that already prohibited discrimination based on sex; they did not purport to "recognize" that sexual orientation discrimination was merely an aspect of already-prohibited discrimination based on sex.

* * *

. . . The above history makes it obvious to me . . . that the majority misconceives the fundamental *public* meaning of the language of the Civil Rights Act. The problem sought to be remedied by adding "sex" to the prohibited bases of employment discrimination was the pervasive discrimination against women in the employment market, and the chosen remedy was to prohibit discrimination that adversely affected members of one sex or the other. By prohibiting discrimination against people based on their sex, it did not, and does not, prohibit discrimination against people because of their sexual orientation.

* * *

The words used in legislation are used for a reason. Legislation is adopted in response to perceived social problems, and legislators adopt the language that they do to address a social evil or accomplish a desirable goal. The words of the statute take meaning from that purpose, and the principles it adopts must be read in light of the problem it was enacted to address. The words may indeed cut deeper than the legislators who voted for the statute fully understood or intended: as relevant here, a law aimed at producing gender equality in the workplace may require or prohibit employment practices that the legislators who voted for it did not yet understand as obstacles to gender equality. Nevertheless, it remains a law aimed at *gender* inequality, and not at other forms of discrimination that were understood at the time, and continue to be understood, as a different kind of prejudice, shared not only by some of those who opposed the rights of women and African-Americans, but also by some who believed in equal rights for women and people of color.

* * *

The majority's linguistic argument does not change the fact that the prohibition of employment discrimination "because of . . . sex" does not protect gays and lesbians. Simply put, discrimination based on sexual orientation is not the same thing as discrimination based on sex. As Judge Sykes explained,

[t]o a fluent speaker of the English language — then and now — the ordinary meaning of the word "sex" does not fairly include the concept of "sexual orientation." The two terms are never used interchangeably, and the latter is not subsumed within the former; there is no overlap in meaning. . . . The words plainly describe different traits, and the separate and distinct meaning of each term is easily grasped. More specifically to the point here, discrimination "because of sex" is not reasonably understood to include discrimination based on sexual orientation, a different immutable characteristic. Classifying people by sexual orientation is different than classifying them by sex.

Hively, 853 F.3d at 363 (Sykes, J., dissenting) (footnote omitted).

* * *

[In addition, the majority's other grounds for finding sex discrimination here are invalid. Stereotypes and association claims are only actionable because they disadvantage one sex. Sexual orientation discrimination does nothing of the kind]. . . .

* * *

. . . When interpreting an act of Congress, we need to respect the choices made by Congress about which social problems to address, and how to address them. In 1964, Congress — belatedly — prohibited employment discrimination based on race, sex, religion, ethnicity, and national origin. Many states have similarly recognized the injustice of discrimination on the basis of sexual orientation. In doing so, they have called such discrimination by its right name, and taken a firm and explicit stand against it. I hope that one day soon Congress will join them, and adopt that principle on a national basis. But it has not done so yet.

For these reasons, I respectfully, and regretfully, dissent.

The history of gender identity and transgender employees under Title VII is similar to that for sexual orientation, but transgender employees had generally had more success beginning in the early 2000s. Like for sexual orientation, the EEOC issued a decision in a federal sector case holding that gender identity discrimination violated Title VII.[110] The Sixth Circuit agreed in the following edited case.

EEOC v. R.G. & G.R. Harris Funeral Homes, Inc.

884 F.3d 560 (6th Cir. 2018).

KAREN NELSON MOORE, Circuit Judge.

Aimee Stephens (formerly known as Anthony Stephens) was born biologically male. While living and presenting as a man, she worked as a funeral director at R.G. & G.R. Harris Funeral Homes, Inc. ("the Funeral Home"), a closely held for-profit corporation that operates three funeral homes in Michigan. Stephens was terminated from the Funeral Home by its owner and operator, Thomas Rost, shortly after Stephens informed Rost that she intended to transition from male to female and would represent herself and dress as a woman while at work. Stephens filed a complaint with the Equal Employment Opportunity Commission ("EEOC"), which investigated Stephens's allegations that she had been terminated as a result of unlawful sex discrimination. . . . The EEOC subsequently brought suit against the Funeral Home in which the EEOC charged the Funeral Home with violating Title VII of the Civil Rights Act of 1964 ("Title VII") by . . . terminating Stephens's employment on the basis of her transgender or transitioning status and her refusal to conform to sex-based stereotypes . . . .

The parties submitted dueling motions for summary judgment. The EEOC argued that it was entitled to judgment as a matter of law on both of its claims. For its part, the Funeral Home argued that it did not violate Title VII by requiring Stephens to comply with a sex-specific dress code that it asserts equally burdens male and female employees, and, in the alternative, that Title VII should not be enforced against the Funeral Home because requiring the Funeral Home to employ Stephens while she dresses and represents herself as a woman would constitute an unjustified substantial burden upon Rost's (and thereby the Funeral Home's) sincerely held religious beliefs, in violation of the Religious Freedom Restoration Act ("RFRA"). . . .

The district court granted summary judgment in favor of the Funeral Home on both claims. For the reasons set forth below, we hold that (1) the Funeral Home engaged in unlawful discrimination against Stephens on the basis of her sex; [and that the Funeral Home is not entitled to a defense under RFRA]. Accordingly, we REVERSE the district court's grant of summary judgment . . . GRANT summary judgment to the EEOC on its unlawful-termination claim,

110. Macy v. Dep't of Justice, EEOC Appeal No. 0120120821 (2012).

and REMAND the case to the district court for further proceedings consistent with this opinion.

* * *

B.   Unlawful Termination Claim

Title VII prohibits employers from "discriminat[ing] against any individual with respect to his compensation, terms, conditions, or privileges of employment, because of such individual's race, color, religion, sex, or national origin." "[A] plaintiff can establish a prima facie case [of unlawful discrimination] by presenting direct evidence of discriminatory intent." "[A] facially discriminatory employment policy or a corporate decision maker's express statement of a desire to remove employees in the protected group is direct evidence of discriminatory intent." Once a plaintiff establishes that "the prohibited classification played a motivating part in the [adverse] employment decision," the employer then bears the burden of proving that it would have terminated the plaintiff "even if it had not been motivated by impermissible discrimination."

Here, the district court correctly determined that Stephens was fired because of her failure to conform to sex stereotypes, in violation of Title VII. The district court erred, however, in finding that Stephens could not alternatively pursue a claim that she was discriminated against on the basis of her transgender and transitioning status. Discrimination on the basis of transgender and transitioning status is necessarily discrimination on the basis of sex, and thus the EEOC should have had the opportunity to prove that the Funeral Home violated Title VII by firing Stephens because she is transgender and transitioning from male to female.

1.   Discrimination on the Basis of Sex Stereotypes

In *Price Waterhouse v. Hopkins*, 490 U.S. 228, 109 S. Ct. 1775 (1989), a plurality of the Supreme Court explained that Title VII's proscription of discrimination *"because of . . .* sex' . . . mean[s] that gender must be irrelevant to employment decisions." In enacting Title VII, the plurality reasoned, "Congress intended to strike at the entire spectrum of disparate treatment of men and women resulting from sex stereotypes." The *Price Waterhouse* plurality, along with two concurring Justices, therefore determined that a female employee who faced an adverse employment decision because she failed to "walk . . . femininely, talk . . . femininely, dress . . . femininely, wear make-up, have her hair styled, [or] wear jewelry," could properly state a claim for sex discrimination under Title VII—even though she was not discriminated against for being a woman per se, but instead for failing to be womanly enough.

Based on *Price Waterhouse*, we determined that "discrimination based on a failure to conform to stereotypical gender norms" was no less prohibited under Title VII than discrimination based on "the biological differences between men and women." *Smith v. City of Salem*, 378 F.3d 566, 573 (6th Cir.2004). And we found no "reason to exclude Title VII coverage for non sex-stereotypical behavior simply because the person is a transsexual." Thus, in *Smith*, we held that a transgender plaintiff (born male) who suffered adverse employment consequences after "he began to express a more feminine appearance and manner on a regular basis" could file an employment discrimination suit under Title VII, because such "discrimination would not [have] occur[red] but for the victim's sex." As we reasoned in *Smith*, Title VII proscribes discrimination both against women who "do not wear dresses or makeup" and men who do. Under any circumstances, "[s]ex stereotyping based on a person's gender non-conforming behavior is impermissible discrimination."

Here, Rost's decision to fire Stephens because Stephens was "no longer going to represent himself as a man" and "wanted to dress as a woman," falls squarely within the ambit of sex-based discrimination that *Price Waterhouse* and *Smith* forbid. For its part, the Funeral Home has failed to establish a non-discriminatory basis for Stephens's termination, and Rost admitted that he did not fire Stephens for any performance-related issues. We therefore agree with the district court that the Funeral Home discriminated against Stephens on the basis of her sex, in violation of Title VII.

The Funeral Home nevertheless argues that it has not violated Title VII because sex stereotyping is barred only when "the employer's reliance on stereotypes . . . result[s] in disparate treatment of employees because they are either male or female." According to the Funeral Home, an employer does not engage in impermissible sex stereotyping when it requires its employees to conform to a sex-specific dress code—as it purportedly did here by requiring Stephens to abide by the dress code designated for the Funeral Home's male employees—because such a policy "impose[s] equal burdens on men and women," and thus does not single out an employee for disparate treatment based on that employee's sex. In support of its position, the Funeral Home relies principally on *Jespersen v. Harrah's Operating Co.*, 444 F.3d 1104 (9th Cir.2006) (en banc) . . . . For three reasons, the Funeral Home's reliance on [this case] is misplaced.

First, the central issue . . . —whether certain sex-specific appearance requirements violate Title VII—is not before this court. We are not considering, in this case, whether the Funeral Home violated Title VII by requiring men to wear pant suits and women to wear skirt suits. Our question is instead whether the Funeral Home could legally terminate Stephens, notwithstanding that she fully intended to comply with the company's sex-specific dress code, simply because she refused to conform to the Funeral Home's notion of her sex. When the Funeral Home's actions are viewed in the proper context, no reasonable jury could believe that Stephens was not "target[ed] . . . for disparate treatment" and that "no sex stereotype factored into [the Funeral Home's] employment decision."

Second, even if we would permit certain sex-specific dress codes in a case where the issue was properly raised, we would not rely on . . . *Jespersen* . . . to do so. . . .

[*Jespersen*] is irreconcilable with our decision in *Smith*. Critical to *Jespersen*'s holding was the notion that the employer's "grooming standards," which required all female bartenders to wear makeup (and prohibited males from doing so), did not on their face violate Title VII because they did "not require [the plaintiff] to conform to a stereotypical image that would objectively impede her ability to perform her job." We reached the exact opposite conclusion in *Smith*, as we explained that requiring women to wear makeup does, in fact, constitute improper sex stereotyping. . . .

Finally, the Funeral Home misreads binding precedent when it suggests that sex stereotyping violates Title VII *only* when "the employer's sex stereotyping resulted in 'disparate treatment of men and women.'" This interpretation of Title VII cannot be squared with our holding in *Smith*. There, we did not ask whether transgender persons transitioning from male to female were treated differently than transgender persons transitioning from female to male. Rather, we considered whether a transgender person was being discriminated against based on "his failure to conform to sex stereotypes concerning how a man should look and behave." It is apparent from both *Price Waterhouse* and *Smith* that an employer engages in unlawful discrimination even if it expects both biologically male and female employees to conform to certain notions of how each should behave. *See Zarda v. Altitude Express, Inc.*, 883 F.3d 100, 123 (2d Cir.2018) (en banc) (plurality) ("[T]he employer in *Price Waterhouse* could not have defended itself by claiming that it fired a gender-nonconforming man as well as a gender-non-conforming woman any more than it could persuasively argue that two wrongs make a right.").

In short, the Funeral Home's sex-specific dress code does not preclude liability under Title VII. Even if the Funeral Home's dress code does not itself violate Title VII—an issue that is not before this court – the Funeral Home may not rely on its policy to combat the charge that it engaged in improper sex stereotyping when it fired Stephens for wishing to appear or behave in a manner that contradicts the Funeral Home's perception of how she should appear or behave based on her sex. Because the EEOC has presented unrefuted evidence that unlawful sex stereotyping was "at least a motivating factor in the [Funeral Home's] actions," and because we reject the Funeral Home's affirmative defenses, we **GRANT** summary judgment to the EEOC on its sex discrimination claim.

2.   Discrimination on the Basis of Transgender/ Transitioning Status

We also hold that discrimination on the basis of transgender and transitioning status violates Title VII. The district court rejected this theory of liability at the motion-to-dismiss stage, holding that "transgender or transsexual status is currently not a protected class under Title VII." The EEOC and Stephens argue that the district court's determination was erroneous because Title VII protects against sex stereotyping and "transgender discrimination is based on the non-conformance of an individual's gender identity and appearance with sex-based norms or expectations"; therefore, "discrimination because of an individual's transgender status is always based on gender-stereotypes: the stereotype that individuals will conform their appearance and behavior—whether their dress, the name they use, or other ways they present themselves—to the sex assigned them at birth." The Funeral Home, in turn, argues that Title VII does not prohibit discrimination based on a person's transgender or transitioning status because "sex," for the purposes of Title VII, "refers to a binary characteristic for which there are only two classifications, male and female," and "which classification arises in a person based on their chromosomally driven physiology and reproductive function." According to the Funeral Home, transgender status refers to "a person's self-assigned 'gender identity'" rather than a person's sex, and therefore such a status is not protected under Title VII.

For two reasons, the EEOC and Stephens have the better argument. First, it is analytically impossible to fire an employee based on that employee's status as a transgender person without being motivated, at least in part, by the employee's sex. The Seventh Circuit's method of "isolat[ing] the significance of the plaintiff's sex to the employer's decision" to determine whether Title VII has been triggered illustrates this point. *See Hively v. Ivy Tech Cmty. Coll. of Ind.*, 853 F.3d 339, 345 (7th Cir. 2017). In *Hively*, the Seventh Circuit determined that Title VII prohibits discrimination on the basis of sexual orientation—a different question than the issue before this court—by asking whether the plaintiff, a self-described lesbian, would have been fired "if she had been a man married to a woman (or living with a woman, or dating a woman) and everything else had stayed the same." If the answer to that question is no, then the plaintiff has stated a "paradigmatic sex discrimination" claim. Here, we ask whether Stephens would have been fired if Stephens had been a woman who sought to comply with the women's dress code. The answer quite obviously is no. This, in and of itself, confirms that Stephens's sex impermissibly affected Rost's decision to fire Stephens.

The court's analysis in *Schroer v. Billington*, 577 F. Supp. 2d 293 (D.D.C.2008), provides another useful way of framing the inquiry. There, the court noted that an employer who fires an employee because the employee converted from Christianity to Judaism has discriminated against the employee "because of religion," regardless of whether the employer feels any animus against either Christianity or Judaism, because "[d]iscrimination 'because of religion' easily encompasses discrimination because of a *change* of religion.'" By the same token, discrimination "because of sex" inherently includes discrimination against employees because of a change in their sex. Here, there is evidence that Rost at least partially based his employment decision on Stephens's desire to change her sex: Rost justified firing Stephens by explaining that Rost "sincerely believes that 'the Bible teaches that a person's sex (whether male or female) is an immutable God-given gift and that it is wrong for a person to deny his or her God-given sex,'" and "the Bible teaches that it is wrong for a biological male to deny his sex by dressing as a woman." As amici point out in their briefing, such statements demonstrate that "Ms. Stephens's sex necessarily factored into the decision to fire her."

The Funeral Home argues that *Schroer*'s analogy is "structurally flawed" because, unlike religion, a person's sex cannot be changed; it is, instead, a biologically immutable trait. We need not decide that issue; even if true, the Funeral Home's point is immaterial. As noted above, the Supreme Court made clear in *Price Waterhouse* that Title VII requires "gender [to] be irrelevant to employment decisions." Gender (or sex) is not being treated as "irrelevant to employment decisions" if an employee's attempt or desire to change his or her sex leads to an adverse employment decision.

Second, discrimination against transgender persons necessarily implicates Title VII's proscriptions against sex stereotyping. As we recognized in *Smith*, a transgender person is someone who "fails to act and/or identify with his or her gender" — i.e., someone who is inherently "gender non-conforming." Thus, an employer cannot discriminate on the basis of transgender status without imposing its stereotypical notions of how sexual organs and gender identity ought to align. There is no way to disaggregate discrimination on the basis of transgender status from discrimination on the basis of gender non-conformity, and we see no reason to try.

. . . [W]e now directly hold: Title VII protects transgender persons because of their transgender or transitioning status, because transgender or transitioning status constitutes an inherently gender non-conforming trait.

The Funeral Home raises several arguments against this interpretation of Title VII, none of which we find persuasive. First, the Funeral Home contends that the Congress enacting Title VII understood "sex" to refer only to a person's "physiology and reproductive role," and not a person's "self-assigned 'gender identity.'" But the drafters' failure to anticipate that Title VII would cover transgender status is of little interpretive value, because "statutory prohibitions often go beyond the principal evil to cover reasonably comparable evils, and it is ultimately the provisions of our laws rather than the principal concerns of our legislators by which we are governed." *Oncale v. Sundowner Offshore Servs., Inc.*, 523 U.S. 75, 79, 118 S. Ct. 998, 1002 (1998); *see also Zarda*, 883 F.3d at 113–16 (majority opinion) (rejecting the argument that Title VII was not originally intended to protect employees against discrimination on the basis of sexual orientation, in part because the same argument "could also be said of multiple forms of discrimination that are [now] indisputably prohibited by Title VII . . . [but] were initially believed to fall outside the scope of Title VII's prohibition," such as "sexual harassment and hostile work environment claims"). And in any event, *Smith* and *Price Waterhouse* preclude an interpretation of Title VII that reads "sex" to mean only individuals' "chromosomally driven physiology and reproductive function." . . .

In a related argument, the Funeral Home notes that both biologically male and biologically female persons may consider themselves transgender, such that transgender status is not unique to one biological sex. It is true, of course, that an individual's biological sex does not dictate her transgender status; the two traits are not coterminous. But a trait need not be exclusive to one sex to nevertheless be a function of sex. As the Second Circuit explained in *Zarda*,

> Title VII does not ask whether a particular sex is discriminated against; it asks whether a particular "*individual*" is discriminated against "because of such *individual's* . . . sex." Taking individuals as the unit of analysis, the question is not whether discrimination is borne only by men or only by women or even by both men and women; instead, the question is whether an individual is discriminated against because of his or her sex.

883 F.3d at 123 n.23 (plurality opinion) (emphasis in original) (quoting 42 U.S.C. § 2000e-2(a)(1)). Because an employer cannot discriminate against an employee for being transgender without considering that employee's biological sex, discrimination on the basis of transgender status necessarily entails discrimination on the basis of sex—no matter what sex the employee was born or wishes to be. By the same token, an employer need not discriminate based on a trait common to all men or women to violate Title VII. After all, a subset of both women and men decline to wear dresses or makeup, but discrimination against any woman on this basis would constitute sex discrimination under *Price Waterhouse*. Nor can much be gleaned from the fact that later statutes, such as the Violence Against Women Act, expressly prohibit discrimination on the basis of "gender identity," while Title VII does not, because "Congress may certainly choose to use both a belt and suspenders to achieve its objectives," *Hively*, 853 F.3d at 344. We have, in fact, already read Title VII to provide redundant statutory protections in a different context. In *In re Rodriguez*, 487 F.3d 1001 (6th Cir.2007), for instance, we recognized that claims alleging discrimination on the basis of ethnicity may fall within Title VII's prohibition on discrimination on the basis of national origin, even though at least one other federal statute treats "national origin" and "ethnicity" as separate traits, *see* 20 U.S.C. § 1092(f)(1)(F)(ii). Moreover, Congress's failure to modify Title VII to include expressly gender identity "lacks 'persuasive significance' because 'several equally tenable inferences' may be drawn from such inaction, 'including the inference that the existing legislation already incorporated the offered change.'" *Pension Benefit Guar. Corp. v. LTV Corp.*, 496 U.S. 633, 650, 110 S. Ct. 2668 (1990) (quoting *United States v. Wise*, 370 U.S. 405, 411, 82 S. Ct. 1354 (1962)). In short, nothing precludes discrimination based on transgender status from being viewed both as discrimination based on "gender identity" for certain statutes and, for the purposes of Title VII, discrimination on the basis of sex.

The Funeral Home places great emphasis on the fact that our published decision in Smith superseded an earlier decision that stated explicitly, as opposed to obliquely, that a plaintiff who "alleges discrimination based solely on his identification as a transsexual . . . has alleged a claim of sex stereotyping pursuant to Title VII." *Smith v. City of Salem*, 369 F.3d 912, 922 (6th Cir.), *opinion amended and superseded*, 378 F.3d 566 (2004). But such an amendment does not mean, as the Funeral Home contends, that the now-binding *Smith* opinion "directly rejected" the notion that Title VII prohibits discrimination on the basis of transgender status. The elimination of the language, which was not necessary to the decision, simply means that *Smith* did not expressly recognize Title VII protections for transgender persons based on identity. But *Smith*'s reasoning still leads us to the same conclusion.

We are also unpersuaded that our decision in *Vickers v. Fairfield Medical Center*, 453 F.3d 757 (6th Cir.2006), precludes the holding we issue today. We held in *Vickers* that a plaintiff cannot pursue a claim for impermissible sex stereotyping on the ground that his perceived sexual orientation fails to conform to gender norms unless he alleges that he was discriminated against for failing to "conform to traditional gender stereotypes in any observable way at work." *Vickers* thus rejected the notion that "the act of identification with a particular group, in itself, is sufficiently gender non-conforming such that an employee who so identifies would, by this very identification, engage in conduct that would enable him to assert a successful sex stereotyping claim." The *Vickers* court reasoned that recognizing such a claim would impermissibly "bootstrap protection for sexual orientation into Title VII." The Funeral Home insists that, under *Vickers*, Stephens's sex-stereotyping claim survives only to the extent that it concerns her "appearance or mannerisms on the job," but not as it pertains to her underlying status as a transgender person.

The Funeral Home is wrong. . . . [W]e are not bound by *Vickers* to the extent that it contravenes *Smith*. . . . The *Vickers* court's new "observable-at-work" requirement is at odds with the holding in *Smith*, which did not limit sex-stereotyping claims to traits that are observable in the workplace. . . . The *Vickers* court's efforts to develop a narrower rule are therefore not binding in this circuit.

Therefore, for the reasons set forth above, we hold that the EEOC could pursue a claim under Title VII on the ground that the Funeral Home discriminated against Stephens on the basis of her transgender status and transitioning identity. The EEOC should have had the opportunity, either through a motion for summary judgment or at trial, to establish that the Funeral Home violated Title VII's prohibition on discrimination on the basis of sex by firing Stephens because she was transgender and transitioning from male to female.

3.   Defenses to Title VII Liability

Having determined that the Funeral Home violated Title VII's prohibition on sex discrimination, we must now consider whether any defenses preclude enforcement of Title VII in this case. As noted above, the district court held that the EEOC's enforcement efforts must give way to the Religious Freedom Restoration Act ("RFRA"), which prohibits the government from enforcing a religiously neutral law against an individual if that law substantially burdens the individual's religious exercise and is not the least restrictive way to further a compelling government interest. [We hold that the Funeral Home has not established that applying Title VII's proscriptions against sex discrimination to it would substantially burden Rost's religious exercise, and therefore the

Funeral Home is not entitled to a defense under RFRA. Even if Rost's religious exercise were substantially burdened, the EEOC has established that enforcing Title VII is the least restrictive means of furthering the government's compelling interest in eradicating workplace discrimination against Stephens].

As the last portion of the opinion states, Rost raised RFRA as a defense, arguing that his religious beliefs motivated his refusal to allow Stephens to follow the dress code for her gender. Because the EEOC brought the claim, the lower court had granted summary judgment to the defendant.[111] The EEOC appealed, and Stephens intervened to ensure that her case could go forward if the EEOC lost.[112] The district court described Rost's religious assertions in the facts of the opinion this way:

> The Funeral Home has been in business since 1910. The Funeral Home is a closely-held, for-profit corporation owned and operated by Thomas Rost ("Rost"). Rost owns 94.5 % of the shares of the Funeral Home. The remaining shares are owned by his children. Rost's grandmother was a funeral director for the business up until 1950. Rost has been the owner of the Funeral Home for over thirty years. Rost has been the President of the Funeral Home for thirty-five years and is the sole officer of the corporation. The Funeral Home has three locations in Michigan: Detroit, Livonia, and Garden City.

> The Funeral Home is not affiliated with or part of any church and its articles of incorporation do not avow any religious purpose. Its employees are not required to hold any religious views. The Funeral Home serves clients of every religion (various Christian denominations, Hindu, Muslim, Jewish, native Chinese religions) or none at all. It employs people from different religious denominations, and of no religious beliefs at all.

* * *

> It is undisputed that Stephens intended to abide by the Funeral Home's dress code for its female employees—which would be to wear a skirt-suit.

> Stephens hand-delivered a copy of [a letter about her transition] to Rost. Rost made the decision to fire Stephens by himself and did so . . . privately . . . in person. Rost testified:

> Q. Okay. How did you fire Stephens: how did you let Ms. Stephens know that she was being released?

> A. Well, I said to him, just before he was—it was right before he was going to go on vacation and I just—I said—I just said "Anthony, this is not going to work out. And that your services would no longer be needed here."

---

111. EEOC v. R.G. & G.R. Harris Funeral Homes, Inc., 884 F.3d 560, 570 (6th Cir. 2018).
112. *Id.*

Stephens also testified that Rost said it was not going to work out. Stephens's understanding from that conversation was that "coming to work dressed as a woman was not going to be acceptable." It was a brief conversation and Stephens left the facility.

* * *

During his deposition in this action, Rost testified:

Q. Okay. Why did you—what was the specific reason that you terminated Stephens?

A. Well, because he—he was no longer going to represent himself as a man. He wanted to dress as a woman.

Q. Okay. So he presented you this letter. . .

A. Number 7, yes.

Q. Yeah, Exhibit 7. So just for a little background and pursuant to the question of Mr. Price, you were presented that letter from Stephens?

A. Correct.

Q. Okay. And did anywhere in that letter indicate that Stephens would continue to dress under your dress code as a man in the workplace?

A. No.

Q. Did he ever tell you during your meeting when he handed you that letter that he would continue to dress as a man?

A. No.

Q. Did he indicate that he would dress as a woman?

A. Yes. Yes.

Q. Okay. Is it—the reason you fired him, was it because he claimed that he was really a woman; is that why you fired him or was it because he claimed—or that he would no longer dress as a man?

A. That he would no longer dress as a man.

Q. And why was that a problem?

A. Well, because we—we have a dress code that is very specific that men will dress as men; in appropriate manner, in a suit and tie that we provide and that women will conform to their dress code that we specify.

Q. So hypothetically speaking, if Stephens had told you that he believed that he was a woman, but would only present as a woman outside of work, would you have terminated him?

A. No.

Rost also testified that the Funeral Home's dress code comports with his religious views.

Rost has been a Christian for over sixty-five years. He attends both Highland Park Baptist Church and Oak Pointe Church. For a time, Rost was on the deacon board of Highland Park Baptist Church. Rost is on the board of the Detroit Salvation Army, a Christian nonprofit ministry, and has been for 15 years; he was the former Chair of the advisory board.

The Funeral Home's mission statement is published on its website, which reads "R.G. & G.R. Harris Funeral Homes recognize that its highest priority is to honor God in all that we do as a company and as individuals. With respect, dignity, and personal attention, our team of caring professionals strive to exceed expectations, offering options and assistance designed to facilitate healing and wholeness in serving the personal needs of family and friends as they experience a loss of life." The website also contains a Scripture verse at the bottom of the mission statement page:

"But seek first his kingdom and righteousness, and all these things shall be yours as well."

Matthew 5:33

In operating the business, Rost places, throughout the funeral homes, Christian devotional booklets called "Our Daily Bread" and small cards with Bible verses on them called "Jesus Cards."

Rost sincerely believes that God has called him to serve grieving people. He sincerely believes that his "purpose in life is to minister to the grieving, and his religious faith compels him to do that important work." It is also undisputed that Rost sincerely believes that the "Bible teaches that a person's sex (whether male or female) is an immutable God-given gift and that it is wrong for a person to deny his or her God-given sex."

In support of the Funeral Home's motion, Rost submitted an affidavit. Rost operates the Funeral Home "as a ministry to serve grieving families while they endure some of the most difficult and trying times in their lives."

At the Funeral Home, the funeral directors are the most "prominent public representatives" of the business and are "the face that [the Funeral Home] presents to the world." The Funeral Home "administers its dress code based on our employees' biological sex, not based on their subjective gender identity."

Rost believes "that the Bible teaches that God creates people male or female." He believes that "the Bible teaches that a person's sex is an immutable God-given gift and that people should not deny or attempt to change their sex." Rost believes that he "would be violating God's commands if [he] were to permit one of the [Funeral Home's] funeral directors to deny their sex while acting as a representative of [the Funeral Home]. This would violate God's commands because, among other reasons, [he] would be directly involved in supporting the idea that sex is a changeable social construct rather than an immutable God-given gift." Rost believes that "the Bible teaches that it is wrong for a biological male to deny his sex by dressing as a woman." Rost believes that he "would be violating God's commands" if he were to permit one of the Funeral Home's male funeral directors to wear the skirt-suit uniform for female directors while at work because Rost "would be directly involved in supporting the idea that sex is a changeable social construct rather than an immutable God-given gift." If Rost "were forced as the owner of [the Funeral Home] to violate [his] sincerely held religious beliefs by paying for or otherwise permitting one of [his] employees to dress inconsistent with his or her biological sex, [Rost] would feel significant pressure to sell [the] business and give up [his] life's calling of ministering to grieving people as a funeral home director and owner."

Rost's Affidavit also states that he "would not have dismissed Stephens if Stephens had expressed [to Rost] a belief that he is a woman and an intent to dress or otherwise present as a woman outside of work, so long as he would have continued to conform to the dress code for male funeral directors while at work. It was Stephens's refusal to wear the prescribed uniform and intent to violate the dress code while at work that was the decisive consideration in [his] employment decision." Rost "would not discharge or otherwise discipline employees who dress as members of the opposite sex on their own time but comply with the dress code while on the job."[113]

The next section considers this and other religiously based defenses to Title VII compliance.

C.   Religious Defenses

Title VII allows some religious employers to discriminate on the basis of religion. It provides

> This title shall not apply . . . to a religious corporation, association, educational institution, or society with respect to the employment of individuals of a particular religion to perform work connected with the carrying on by such corporation, association, educational institution, or society of its activities.[114]

Courts had held that for-profit companies were not considered religious organizations for purposes of this provision.[115] But that was before *Burwell*

---

113. EEOC v. R.G. & G.R. Harris Funeral Homes, Inc., 201 F. Supp. 837, 843-48 (E.D. Mich. 2016).

114. 42 U.S.C. § 2000e-1(a) (2012).

115. *E.g.,* EEOC v. Townley Eng'g & Mfg. Co., 859 F.2d 610 (9th Cir. 1988); *cf.* Spencer v. World Vision, Inc., 633 F.3d 723 (9th Cir. 2011).

v. Hobby Lobby Stores, Inc.,[116] which held that closely held corporations whose shareholders had religious views were "persons" for purposes of the Religious Freedom Act's protections. It is unclear whether that decision will affect the definition of religious organizations under Title VII; no court has yet considered the issue head on. The closest a court has come was in *EEOC v. R.G. & G.R. Harris Funeral Homes, Inc.*[117] There, although the employer only relied on RFRA as a defense, amici had argued that the funeral home was exempt from Title VII because it was a religious organization[118]—this argument was raised in the context of the ministerial exception, but the test for whether an entity is a religious institution is similar, and it is the first step to the ministerial exception analysis. There, because "the Funeral Home 'is not affiliated with any church; its articles of incorporation do not avow any religious purpose; its employees are not required to hold any particular religious views; and it employs and serves individuals of all religions,'" it was not a religious institution.[119] Additionally, it engaged in no public displays of faith, did not decorate its rooms with religious images, and was open every day, including Christian holidays. The court did not rely on the Funeral Home's for-profit status, however.[120]

Whether an employer will qualify as a religious organization is fact intensive, but not overly broad. The organization must be focused on religious activities, but does not have to be a traditional religious organization, like a church—it just has to be "religiously affiliated" with a mission "marked by clear or obvious religious characteristics."[121] Similarly, whether an educational institution will qualify is based on the institution's current religious activities, focus of the curriculum, affiliation of students and faculty, and history and mission of the school. Founding by a religious order, close affiliation, or some religious orientation alone won't ensure that the institution hasn't evolved into a secular institution.[122]

A religious organization can discriminate in employment not only on the basis of religious faith or church membership, but also to penalize behavior that conflicts with the religious tenets of the religious organization employer.[123] As you might guess, this has set up a potential conflict within Title VII—a conflict that was foreshadowed by the *Harris Funeral*

116. 573 U.S. 682 (2014).
117. 884 F.3d 560 (6th Cir. 2018).
118. *Id.* at 581.
119. *Id.* at 582.
120. *Id.* at 582-83.
121. Conlon v. InterVarsity Christian Fellowship, 777 F.3d 829, 834 (6th Cir. 2015).
122. EEOC v. Kamehameha Schs., 990 F.2d 458 (9th Cir. 1993).
123. Curay-Cramer v. Ursuline Acad. of Wilmington, 450 F.3d 130 (3d Cir. 2006) (public support of the right of women to secure an abortion); Killinger v. Samford Univ., 113 F.3d 196 (11th Cir. 1997) (criticism of fundamentalist theology); Little v. Wuerl, 929 F.2d 944 (3d Cir. 1991) (remarriage after divorce).

Homes case. Some religions consider sex to be something fixed and binary, as a matter of faith, and some condemn same sex intimate behavior. So does that mean a religious organization can discriminate on the basis of sexual orientation and gender identity even if for other kinds of employers, doing so is sex discrimination? The Supreme Court has not answered that question, but the cases cited above and others like them suggest that employers may be able to.

The Department of Justice took this position in a *Memorandum on Religious Liberty*, issued in 2017:

> Section 702 broadly exempts from its reach religious corporations, associations, educational institutions, and societies. The statute's terms do not limit this exemption to non-profit organizations, to organizations that carry on only religious activities, or to organizations established by a church or formally affiliated therewith. *See* Civil Rights Act of 1964, § 702(a), codified at 42 U.S.C. § 2000e-1(a); *see also Hobby Lobby*, 134 S. Ct. at 2773-74; Corp. of Presiding Bishop, 483 U.S. at 335-36. The exemption applies whenever the organization is "religious," which means that it is organized for religious purposes and engages in activity consistent with, and in furtherance of, such purposes. Br. of Amicus Curiae the U.S. Supp. Appellee, *Spencer v. World Vision, Inc.*, No. 08-35532 (9th Cir. 2008). Thus, the exemption applies not just to religious denominations and houses of worship, but to religious colleges, charitable organizations like the Salvation Army and World Vision International, and many more. In that way, it is consistent with other broad protections for religious entities in federal law, including, for example, the exemption of religious entities from many of the requirements under the Americans with Disabilities Act. *See* 28 C.F.R. app. C; 56 Fed. Reg. 35544, 35554 (July 26, 1991) (explaining that "[t]he ADA's exemption of religious organizations and religious entities controlled by religious organizations is very broad, encompassing a wide variety of situations").
>
> In addition to these explicit exemptions, religious organizations may be entitled to additional exemptions from discrimination laws. *See, e.g., Hosanna-Tabor*, 565 U.S. at 180, 188-90 [excerpted below]. For example, a religious organization might conclude that it cannot employ an individual who fails faithfully to adhere to the organization's religious tenets, either because doing so might itself inhibit the organization's exercise of religion or because it might dilute an expressive message. *Cf. Boy Scouts of Am. v. Dale*, 530 U.S. 640, 649-55 (2000). Both constitutional and statutory issues arise when governments seek to regulate such decisions.
>
> As a constitutional matter, religious organizations' decisions are protected from governmental interference to the extent they relate to ecclesiastical or internal governance matters. *Hosanna-Tabor*, 565 U.S. at 180, 188-90. It is beyond dispute that "it would violate the First Amendment for courts to apply [employment discrimination] laws to compel the ordination of women by the Catholic Church or by an Orthodox Jewish seminary." *Id.* at 188. The same is true for other employees who "minister to the faithful," including those who are not themselves the head of the religious congregation and

who are not engaged solely in religious functions. *Id.* at 188, 190, 194-95; *see also* Br. of Amicus Curiae the U.S. Supp. Appellee, *Spencer v. World Vision, Inc.*, No. 08-35532 (9th Cir. 2008) (noting that the First Amendment protects "the right to employ staff who share the religious organization's religious beliefs"). Even if a particular associational decision could be construed to fall outside this protection, the government would likely still have to show that any interference with the religious organization's associational rights is justified under strict scrutiny. *See Roberts v. U.S. Jaycees*, 468 U.S. 609, 623 (1984) (infringements on expressive association are subject to strict scrutiny); *Smith*, 494 U.S. at 882 ("[I]t is easy to envision a case in which a challenge on freedom of association grounds would likewise be reinforced by Free Exercise Clause concerns."). The government may be able to meet that standard with respect to race discrimination, see *Bob Jones Univ.*, 461 U.S. at 604, but may not be able to with respect to other forms of discrimination. For example, at least one court has held that forced inclusion of women into a mosque's religious men's meeting would violate the freedom of expressive association. *Donaldson v. Farrakhan*, 762 N.E.2d 835, 840-41 (Mass. 2002). The Supreme Court has also held that the government's interest in addressing sexual-orientation discrimination is not sufficiently compelling to justify an infringement on the expressive association rights of a private organization. *Boy Scouts*, 530 U.S. at 659.

As a statutory matter, RFRA too might require an exemption or accommodation for religious organizations from antidiscrimination laws. For example, "prohibiting religious organizations from hiring only coreligionists can 'impose a significant burden on their exercise of religion, even as applied to employees in programs that must, by law, refrain from specifically religious activities.'" Application of the Religious Freedom Restoration Act to the Award of a Grant Pursuant to the Juvenile Justice and Delinquency Prevention Act, 31 Op. O.L.C. 162, 172 (2007) (quoting Direct Aid to Faith-Based Organizations Under the Charitable Choice Provisions of the Community Solutions Act of 2001, 25 Op. O.L.C. 129, 132 (2001)); *see also Corp. of Presiding Bishop*, 483 U.S. at 336 (noting that it would be "a significant burden on a religious organization to require it, on pain of substantial liability, to predict which of its activities a secular court w[ould] consider religious" in applying a nondiscrimination provision that applied only to secular, but not religious, activities). If an organization establishes the existence of such a burden, the government must establish that imposing such burden on the organization is the least restrictive means of achieving a compelling governmental interest. That is a demanding standard and thus, even where Congress has not expressly exempted religious organizations from its antidiscrimination laws-as it has in other contexts, *see, e.g.*, 42 U.S.C. §§ 3607 (Fair Housing Act), 12187 (Americans with Disabilities Act) – RFRA might require such an exemption.[124]

---

124. Memorandum on Federal Law Protections for Religious Liberty 12a-13a (Oct. 6, 2017), https://www.justice.gov/opa/press-release/file/1001891/download

Following the guidance in this memorandum, the Department of Labor proposed a new rule in August on discrimination by religious organizations.[125] The Department, through the Office of Federal Corporate Compliance Programs, enforces Executive Order 11246, which prohibits discrimination on the basis of sex, sexual orientation, and gender identity (among other characteristics) by federal contractors. The proposed rule first makes clear that religious organizations can discriminate on the basis of religion and that religion is not just belief but also religious practices.[126] So, religious organizations can require employees to conform their behavior to the organization's religiously motivated rules. In defining religion, the proposed rule draws on Title VII and adopts definitions from the Religious Freedom Restoration Act and Religious Land Use and Institutionalized Persons Act.[127]

Second, it defines what counts as a "religious corporation, association, educational institution, or society." The key changes are to what counts as a religious corporation. The EEOC's guidance has long provided that for-profit entities cannot be religious organizations for purposes of Title VII, taking the definition from court decisions. The proposed rule removes that limitation, citing the *Hobby Lobby* case and suggesting that Hobby Lobby would be considered a religious corporation—despite the fact that the question in *Hobby Lobby* was whether corporations were persons for purposes of the Religious Freedom Restoration Act.[128] Title VII does not use "person," so the logic does not necessarily apply. Now, a religious organization will be any entity including a for-profit corporation that:

1. is organized for a religious purpose;
2. holds itself out to the public as carrying out a religious purpose; and
3. exercises religion consistent with and in furtherance of a religious purpose.[129]

One limitation in the proposed rule is this sentence: "With that said, OFCCP does not see a scenario in which an entity's single religiously motivated employment action, standing alone, would be sufficient to satisfy [the third] element of the definition, if that were the only religiously motivated action the entity could identify."[130]

The proposed rule states that this does not allow federal contractors to discriminate on bases other than religion, but then says "where a contractor that is entitled to the religious exemption claims that its challenged

125. 84 Fed. Reg. 41677 (Aug. 15, 2019).
126. *Id.* at 41679.
127. *Id.* at 41679, 41684.
128. *Id.* at 41684.
129. *Id.* at 41682-83.
130. *Id.* at 41683.

employment action was based on religion, OFCCP will find a violation of Executive Order 11246 only if it can prove by a preponderance of the evidence that a protected characteristic other than religion was a but-for cause of the adverse action,"[131] citing *University of Texas Southwest Medical Center v. Nassar*[132] and *Gross v. FBL Financial Services, Inc.*,[133] despite the fact that those cases involved retaliation and the ADEA, respectively, not the status discrimination provision of Title VII. Although the OFCCP had previously adopted the motivating factor causation standard from Title VII in prior notice-and-comment-rulemaking,[134] it rejected that standard for religious employers, reasoning that a mixed motives causation standard, "could require OFCCP to enter the Constitutionally suspect minefield of having to evaluate the nature of a sincerely held belief, which could result in the inappropriate encroachment upon the organization's religious integrity."[135]

This certainly tees up conflicts with protection against sex discrimination versus religious beliefs of employers, particularly when it comes to pregnancy and sexual minorities.

D.   The Gender Pay Gap

The Ninth Circuit made news when it decided *Rizo v. Yozino*,[136] a case about the meaning of "any other factor other than sex" in the Equal Pay Act, en banc. The case involved the Fresno County Office of Education, which based a new employee's entering salary solely on her prior salary plus 5%.[137] After Aileen Rizo was hired, she discovered that male co-workers with the same job were paid more than she was and sued.[138]

The only question on appeal was whether an employee's prior salary was "any other factor other than sex" such that an employer could base salary decisions on it without running afoul of the Equal Pay Act's prohibition on paying men and women different wages.[139] The majority said prior salary was not a factor other than sex for two primary reasons. First, if prior salary were a factor other than sex, then that exception would allow employers to rely on discriminatory wages set by prior employers, perpetuating sex

131. *Id.* at 41685.
132. 570 U.S. 338, 362–63 (2013).
133. 557 U.S. 167, 180 (2009).
134. 80 Fed. Reg. 54934, 54944–46 (Sept. 11, 2015).
135. *Id.* at 41685 n.10.
136. 887 F.3d 453 (9th Cir. 2018), *vacated* 139 S. Ct. 706 (2019).
137. *Id.* at 457.
138. *Id.* at 458.
139. *Id.* at 460.

discrimination and undermining the Equal Pay Act's purpose.[140] Second, the list of affirmative defenses prior to the any-other-factor affirmative defense all related to job-related factors that, as the legislative history demonstrated, Congress recognized would justify different wages: seniority, a merit system, and productivity.[141] Accordingly, and because motive is not relevant in equal pay act cases, "any other factor other than sex" must be limited to job-related factors.[142] Prior salary may be based on job-related factors, but employers must discover what those factors were and rely on them rather than simply using that salary as a proxy for those factors — that proxy is a poor fit and may too easily embody discrimination. In the court's words:

> Prior salary does not fit within the catchall exception because it is not a legitimate measure of work experience, ability, performance, or any other job-related quality. It may bear a rough relationship to legitimate factors other than sex, such as training, education, ability, or experience, but the relationship is attenuated. More important, it may well operate to perpetuate the wage disparities prohibited under the Act. Rather than use a second-rate surrogate that likely masks continuing inequities, the employer must instead point directly to the underlying factors for which prior salary is a rough proxy, at best, if it is to prove its wage differential is justified under the catchall exception.[143]

There were three concurring opinions. All of the judges agreed that relying solely on prior salary at a previous employer to set a starting salary ran afoul of the EPA because of the danger that the prior salary was based on sex.[144] The concurring judges would have accepted prior salary as one factor in the mix,[145] however, essentially believing that prior salary was likely based mostly on legitimate job-related factors.

This opinion marked a clear split among the circuits on this issue. The Seventh Circuit has held that prior salary is always factor other than sex,[146] while the Ninth with this case said it never is. The other circuits and the EEOC fall somewhere in the middle — more in line with the concurrences,

---

140. *Id.* at 460-61.
141. *Id.* at 461-62.
142. *Id.* at 462-64.
143. *Id.* at 467.
144. *Id.* at 469-70 (McKeown, J., concurring); *id.* at 477 (Callahan, J., concurring); *id.* at 479 (Watford, J., concurring).
145. *Id.* at 470-71 (McKeown, J., concurring); *id.* at 473-77 (Callahan, J., concurring); *id.* at 478-79 (Watford, J., concurring).
146. Wernsing v. Dep't of Human Servs., 427 F.3d 466, 468-70 (7th Cir. 2005).

that prior salary can be considered as just one factor as long as it is combined with other job-related factors.[147]

Reading all of the opinions is well worth the time it takes. They thoroughly and clearly summarize the state of the law on the "any factor other than sex" defense. They also very effectively explain the disagreements over causes of the gender wage gap, what kind of employer action constitutes discrimination, and what role the law should play. For example, one of the main points of disagreement seems to be whether the Equal Pay Act ought to be treated like disparate treatment in pay under Title VII. In other words, is motive required for a pay differential to be because of sex? And is the persistent gender pay gap caused by that kind of motive, or is it based on other factors that are not attributable to an employer's bad motive? Moreover, should the government intervene in cases without bad motives?

Unfortunately, the Supreme Court granted certiorari in the case and vacated the opinion, although it did not reverse the result.[148] The majority opinion had been written by Judge Reinhardt, who died eleven days before the opinion was published, and without him, the opinion he wrote was joined by only five of the ten members of the en banc court.[149] The Ninth Circuit had noted that the opinion was written and the votes held before Judge Reinhardt died, but the Supreme Court found that reasoning insufficient to count his vote, noting that "it is generally understood that a judge may change his or her position up to the very moment when a decision is released."[150] The Court concluded,

> Because Judge Reinhardt was no longer a judge at the time when the en banc decision in this case was filed, the Ninth Circuit erred in counting him as a member of the majority. That practice effectively allowed a deceased judge to exercise the judicial power of the United States after his death. But federal judges are appointed for life, not for eternity.[151]

147. EEOC Compliance Manual, Compensation Discrimination § 10-IV.F.2.g (2000), https://www.eeoc.gov/policy/docs/compensation.html; Riser v. QEP Energy, 776 F.3d 1191, 1199 (10th Cir. 2015) (allowing former salary to be considered as one of many factors); Irby v. Bittick, 44 F.3d 949, 955 (11th Cir. 2015) (prior salary can be considered if it is linked with differences in experience); Drum v. Leeson Elec. Corp., 565 F.3d 1071, 1073 (8th Cir. 2009) (carefully examining the evidence submitted by the employer to ensure it could actually explain why the woman's salary was below market rates for the position she was hired for); Aldrich v. Randolph Central Sch. Dist., 963 F.2d 520, 526 (2d Cir. 1992) (holding that an employer must prove that a bona fide business-related reason exists for using the gender-neutral factor that results in a wage differential); *see* EEOC v. J.C. Penney Co. Inc., 843 F.2d 249, 253 (6th Cir. 1988) (recognizing that a "legitimate business reason" for different pay will satisfy the standard).

148. Yovino v. Rizo, 139 S. Ct. 706 (2019) (per curiam).

149. *Id.* at 707-08.

150. *Id.* at 709.

151. *Id.* at 710.

The last year saw a number of additional pay gap developments. At the federal level, the EEOC appears to be abandoning efforts to collect data on pay and hours of employees to better study disparities. The EEOC has announced that it would not request to renew enhanced data it is collecting this year for the first time on hours and pay of employees.[152] Known as Component 2 of the EEO-1 form that large employers must submit to the EEOC annually, the enhanced data collection was controversial. The Trump administration had blocked the enhanced data collection before it began.[153] The National Women's Law Center sued to reinstate the data collection and won, the court ordering reinstatement of the data collection rule in March.[154] Thus, data will be collected for one year, but not again until the EEOC requests to renew its collection.

The Paycheck Fairness Act passed the House in March 2019.[155] That legislation would amend the Equal Pay Act to:

1. change the "any other factor other than sex" defense to require "a bona fide factor other than sex, such as education, training, or experience" and put limits on what an employer must prove;
2. enhance retaliation prohibitions;
3. make it unlawful to require an employee to sign a contract or waiver prohibiting the employee from disclosing information about the employee's wages; and
4. increase civil penalties for violations of equal pay provisions.

The Senate version was referred to the Committee on Health, Education, Labor, and Pensions,[156] but there is little chance that it will move forward in the current political climate.[157]

The states have been very active in this area as well.[158] A good summary of legislation over the last few years can be found in Erin Connell and Kathryn G. Mantoan's article, *Mind the Gap: Pay Audits, Pay Transparency, and Its Public Disclosure of Pay Data* in the ABA Journal of Labor & Employment

---

152. 84 Fed. Reg. 48138 (Sept. 12, 2019).

153. Nat'l Women's Law Ctr. v. Office of Mgmt. & Budget, 358 F. Supp. 66, 74-75 (D.D.C. 2019).

154. *Id.* at 92-93.

155. H.R. 7, 116th Cong. (2019).

156. S. 270, 116th Cong. (2019).

157. Jaclyn Diaz, *States Look to Remedy Pay Gap as Federal Legislation Stalls*, BLOOMBERG LAW DAILY LABOR REPORT (July 31, 2019, 9:38 AM), https://news.bloomberglaw.com/daily-labor-report/states-look-to-remedy-the-pay-gap-as-federal-legislation-stalls.

158. *See id.* (noting laws in eleven states that will go into effect in 2019).

Law.[159] The National Women's Law Center also issued a brief update in 2018, that identified key areas of legislative reform:

- Pay transparency
- Prohibiting the use of salary history
- Expanding protections beyond sex
- Requiring equal pay for "substantially similar" or "comparable" work
- Limiting employer defenses
- Focusing on promotions and advancement opportunities
- Expanding limitations periods for bringing legal action
- Increasing remedies
- Requiring more from contractors to ensure compliance.[160]

---

159. Erin Connell & Kathryn G. Mantoan, *Mind the Gap: Pay Audits, Pay Transparency, and Its Public Disclosure of Pay Data*, 33 ABA J. LAB. & EMP. L. 1 (2018).

160. NAT'L WOMEN'S LAW CTR., PROGRESS IN THE STATS FOR EQUAL PAY (2018), https://nwlc-ciw49tixgw5lbab.stackpathdns.com/wp-content/uploads/2018/06/Progress-in-the-States-for-Equal-Pay-2018-1.pdf.

www.ingramcontent.com/pod-product-compliance
Lightning Source LLC
Chambersburg PA
CBHW061840220326
41599CB00027B/5348